Syria on the Path to Economic Reform

St Andrews Papers on Contemporary Syria

SERIES EDITOR, RAYMOND HINNEBUSCH

Syria on the Path to Economic Reform

Samir Seifan

University of St Andrews Centre for Syrian Studies

Published by the University of St Andrews Centre for Syrian Studies
School of International Relations
Fife, Scotland
UK

Distributed throughout the world by
Lynne Rienner Publishers, Inc.
1800 30th Street
Boulder, CO 80301
USA
www.rienner.com

British Library Cataloguing-in-Publication Data
A catalogue record for this book is available from the British Library

Printed and bound in the United States of America

ISBN: 978-0-9559687-6-1

Contents

Foreword
Raymond Hinnebusch

In this volume, Syria's most prominent development economist delivers a judicious and detailed assessment of Syria's road to economic reform. This is based on his intimate experience with the political economy of the country over many years, including his participation in the preparation of numerous reports on reform for the government, private sector and international institutions. Seifan remains an independent economist and social thinker, who, however, accepts the board limits of the regime's reform project while asking what its actual results have been and what would be needed if it were to achieve its stated aim of a 'social market economy'— a market economy that avoids the extremes of inequality from unregulated capitalism.

In the first essay in the volume, he traces the process of Syria's reform, the forces pushing and obstructing it, and the debates and options considered by policymakers. He explains the regime's reluctance to lay out a detailed plan of reform from a fear it would coalesce opposition and a sense that, feeling its way by experiment, its path must not be straitjacketed; the cost is that confidence, notably among investors, in the durability and direction of reform remains shallow. He shows, however, that the decision for reform is irreversible, at least in its broad lines, and lays out in detail the steps and consequences of reform in the first decade of Bashar al-Asad's presidency.

In the second part of the volume, switching from descriptive/analytical mode to prescriptive, Seifan lays out a plausible model of the "Social Market" economy the regime ostensibly seeks to create. He locates this model within the context of debates in Syria and identifies a tendency for the 'reformists' in government to uncritically adopt the viewpoint of neo-liberalism that social welfare provisions merely detract from investment and growth and must be sacrificed to the need to restart a capitalist economy. In theoretical terms, he situates the social market model between the failures of statism and the perils of extreme neo-liberalism, arguing for a mixed economy, in which, not only would the state regulate the market, provide a minimum of welfare, and organize capital-labor relations, but also would foster a widespread distribution of property, notably cooperatives and small enterprises, while at the same time encouraging the adoption of value-added industries and the formation of a more skilled labor force through investment in human capital.

Lastly, the appendix contains the proceedings of a conference, "Syria in a Changing World" (held in Damascus in November 2008 jointly by the Centre for Syrian Studies and the Orient Institute of Studies) which provides a formidable example of the vivid debate on economic reform in Syria.

From this volume, the reader will learn much about the political economy of reform in Syria, will be sensitized to the debates over the process and will benefit from a wealth of detail on specific outcomes after several years of reform.

1
The Reform Paradox in Syria

The history of reform before 2000

The blockage of Syria's first opening

Syria's foreign policy and its domestic economic policy are inextricably linked. Few people would realize that Syria had prepared to return to a capitalist market economy as early as after the October war in 1973: During that period, the economy was opened on a larger scale, Syria allowed the first foreign (American) oil company to operate in the country, US President Nixon visited Damascus in 1974 and Syria received considerable assistance from the pro-Western oil-producing countries in the Arab world while some tensions appeared in relations with the eastern bloc. The opening towards private investment gained momentum and the Syrian-Western rapprochement was crowned by Syria's entrance into Lebanon in 1976 with French and American blessing to stop the civil war which had erupted in 1975. During the first stages of intervention, Syria sided with the pro-west "rightist forces" and clashed with the Palestinians and pro-Palestinian Lebanese "national" forces.

However, foreign policy returned Syria to its original tangent after President Sadat visited Jerusalem in 1977 and signed the Camp David agreement in 1978. Syria opposed the bilateral peace signed by Sadat and called for a comprehensive peace agreement between the Arabs and Israel. Another significant event that played a decisive role in Syria's political and economic orientation was the Muslim Brotherhood insurgency of the late 1970s/early 1980s which received direct financial and moral support from a considerable part of the Syrian business sector, and some of the conservative Arab monarchies as well as moral support from the western media and US officials, with western countries providing asylum to Brotherhood leaders. The United States listed Syria among the terrorism-sponsoring countries in 1979 and the pro-Western Arab countries started to reduce their financial contributions to Syria. All the preceding factors contributed to the economic crisis that erupted in the second half of the 1980s. But their immediate impact was to improve relations with the eastern bloc countries crowned by the signing of the Syrian-Soviet Friendship Agreement in 1980. In Lebanon, where approximately 40,000 Syrian soldiers were deployed, Syria revised its position and allied with the Palestinians. The limited Israeli invasion of Lebanon in 1978 followed by the second invasion in 1982 and the direct clash with Syrian troops, that ended with the Israel occupation of southern Lebanon for 18 years, until 2000, consolidated Syrian opposition to western policy in the region. Here also, political events impacted on economic developments.

Syria halted the limited economic opening of the mid 1970s toward the private sector, and revived such slogans as "the leading role of the public sector." As a result, the inflow of Arab capital began to diminish from the early 1980s and the investment climate in Syria became less and less attractive. Syrian capital continued to exit the country and government spending exceeded fiscal revenues, which prompted deficit spending by direct borrowing from the Syrian Central Bank. Between 1976 – 1980 the state budget deficit reached around 49% and government to the central bank went from 6 billion SP in 1976 to 74 billion in 1986. The money supply grew around 27% between 1975 and 1985 whereas GDP grew only 14.5%. The reserve of hard currency and gold went down to 2% where the minimum limit is 10% according the currency law. The country's foreign reserves hit bottom in 1987. This in turn forced the government to stop financing many public enterprises, whose production halted or declined sharply. Public as well as private job opportunities receded and unemployment emerged as a socioeconomic problem. These problems reached crisis proportions after 1986 as indicated by the rapid depreciation of the Syrian pound against foreign currencies. The dollar price rose from SYP 3.90 in 1079 to SYP 5.52 in 1980, around SYP 10 in 1985, SYP 20 in 1986 and SYP 45 by the end of the 1980s. This was associated with a big increase in inflation levels which reached 15-25% or higher, resulting in increased prices and deteriorating purchasing power of groups living on fixed incomes, consequently affecting the living standards of most Syrians. Shortages of goods and services became familiar and essential items disappeared from the market such as vegetable oil, margarine, sugar, tea and coffee. Smuggling became widespread especially across the Syrian-Lebanese borders. Illicit enrichment widened and parasitic capitalists thrived by exploiting relations with decision-making centers. The regime deliberately tolerated or encouraged such corruption to secure the loyalty of segments of the bourgeoisie and key regime figures in its struggle against the Muslim Brotherhood. It rewarded Damascus businessmen for their loyalty during the struggle while it punished Aleppo for siding with the

Muslim Brotherhood. In the same period, a bureaucratic bourgeoisie emerged among high ranking state officials and managers and the political and military leaderships.

Limited reforms after the mid-1980s crisis

The intensifying internal economic crisis was paralleled by the 1985 launching of perestroika in the Soviet Union and communist East Europe in which these countries tried to revive their private sectors. Simultaneously, Soviet political support to Syria started to decline. These developments encouraged a revival of liberal economic thinking in Syria. The government, unable to confront the crisis by itself, felt the need to promote the private sector to assume part of the economic burden, despite its suspicion of private capital. Syria, despite the 1960s nationalizations, has always maintained an active private sector. Agriculture remained private except for some state farms; private manufacturing industries had regained growth since the 1970s; land transport, contracting, and domestic trade remained in the hands of the private sector with only a limited role by public institutions; and the private artisan sector remained widespread. Amidst the crisis, Syria took some steps toward further opening to the private sector although they were ad hoc measures to relieve the crisis and not built on a comprehensive concept or integrated vision of economic reform. The government widened the scope for private enterprises and ceded some of its monopolies in foreign trade. Decree 186 of 1985 by the Higher Council for Tourism promoted investment in tourism through limited tax exemptions and facilitating the import of tourist requirements and dealing in foreign currencies. Then Law 10 of 1986 was issued to promote joint agricultural investment between the state (that provides land) and the private sector (that provides capital). Overall, the private sector contribution to GDP increased from a low of 30% in the 1960s to 37% in 1980 (today it is around 65%).

Syria had, since the beginning of the Perestroika, tried to approach the West. The question for the Syrian leadership was how to do so at an affordable price. The opportunity came with the second Gulf war when Syria joined the international coalition under American leadership against Iraq, and thereafter through its participation in the Madrid peace conference. This external realignment was followed by a further internal opening up, crowned by Law 10 of 1991 which constituted the cornerstone of all liberalization steps before 2001. All these cumulative measures attracted a wave of investments in the first half of the 1990s, in particular in the fields of industry and transport.

The economic crisis was greatly eased in the first half of the 1990s by a combination of factors. First, Syria's participation in the second Gulf War was rewarded by the US, Saudi Arabia and the Gulf countries with an inflow of financial support, easy loans and facilitated entry of Syrian labor to the Gulf countries. Second, increased oil production from new fields discovered by Royal Dutch Shell in 1985 in Deir Ezzor and French Elf-Aquitaine when added to that of the Syrian Petroleum Company brought total production from 170,000 barrel per day (b/d) in 1985 to 408,000 b/d in 1990 and over 620,000 b/d in 1996 before it decreased to 556,000 b/d in 2000 and 360,000 b/d in 2005. Second the regime's agriculture support policy paid off: subsidizing the prices of products bought from local farmers (wheat, barley, cotton, sugar beet, lentil and chickpea), at levels higher than global prices, provision of seeds, fertilizers and medicines at subsidized prices and making available easy, long/short term agricultural loans (in kind and in cash) transformed Syria into a country with a constantly growing agricultural surplus. Syria became a wheat exporter after being a wheat importer in the 1980s and wheat is an essential component in the diet of the poor. Fourth, increased opportunities were given to the private sector, with state import monopolies relinquished and imports facilitated by allowing the use of "export proceeds currency" to cover import costs. This, however, eased the subsidy pressure on the state treasury and shifted it to citizens, and increased prices, leading to deteriorating living standards especially for state employees, turning middle-income groups into low-income groups.

The problem was that the government did not follow up Law 10 with any further reforms or articulate a broader reform program with the result that investment slowed down. Further reform was deterred by the easing of the economic crisis but also by fears for political stability. Empowering the private sector would lead the bourgeoisie to seek political power as it had done in the 1980s when it supported the Muslim Brotherhood insurgency. The instability unleashed by economic reform in Eastern Europe and Algeria also induced caution in Syria. As a result investors' enthusiasm cooled down causing an investment recession as of 1995, which slowed economic growth, falling to minus growth in 1999 which was coupled with higher levels of population growth, unemployment and capital drain. Syria had fallen again into economic crisis. Starting in 1998, the regime reversed years of antagonism to Iraq and tried to benefit from the situation there by developing economic ties. This helped alleviate the economic crisis but this temporary relief would be closed off by the American occupation of Iraq in 2003. In retrospect, the failure to consolidate the economic reforms prefigured by Law 10 with new measures led to the perception of the 1990s as a lost decade. However, this experience had a lasting effect on pro-reform currents inside the regime whose attitude towards reform turned by the end of the decade from "caution" into "support".

Economic reform under President Bashar Al-Asad

On June 10th, 2000, President Hafez Al-Assad died after having ruled Syria for three decades (16/11/1970 to 10/6/2000). A smooth transfer of power took place in a referendum in July 2000, when his son Bashar was elected president for a 7-year term. Seven years later, on May 27, 2007 a second referendum was conducted for a new 7-year term, which will last till summer 2014. Economic reform assumed comprehensive and stable characteristics during the first presidential term.

Bashar's first inauguration speech stressed the need for "a comprehensive development strategy providing a specific framework for steps and measures to be taken to achieve this strategy." The speech also set out strategic guidelines for "taking steady and firm steps, albeit piecemeal, towards...economic change." The speech seemed to promise change, and Syrians were hopeful after decades of an authoritarian-run statist economy. While promising change, the speech focused on the technical aspects of the reform process without specifying an economic orientation or the nature of economic system that would result. It only mentioned enhancing private investment while maintaining but reforming the public sector.

For many reasons, the approach of the government was to push dialogue and action towards economic rather than political reform. The first step was the creation of the "Committee of 18", named after the 18 Syrian economists who prepared the first report about the state economy and means of reform. The report did not lead to any practical applications and was perhaps aimed at initiating dialogue about new ideas of economic reform in Syria. In the spring of 2001, the "Committee of 35" was set up to discuss means to reform the public industrial sector. It recommended financial and administrative autonomy to allow sufficient flexibility for the sector to work within a competitive market environment. However, its recommendations again were not implemented. In June 2002, a ministerial committee developed an economic reform draft. As a result, large-scale discussions were initiated involving the government, the Baath Party, economic experts, the interested public and local media. The 9-month discussions led to setting up a 7-expert technical committee on February 25, 2003, by virtue of a decision by Prime Minister Mustapha Miro to redraft the economic reform program. It completed this task within three months and presented its report to the Prime Minister. The report was brushed aside like previous programs and reports. Again, when the French government delegated a number of teams to study the situation in Syria between 2003 and 2004 and to propose administrative and judicial reforms, their recommendations were not implemented although this did result in establishing a branch of the National Institute of Public Administration (INA); a well known French institute for qualifying civil service middle managers. It appears that the purpose of these committees and reports was to open discussions about needed change and to prepare the state institutions and society to accept them.

The American occupation of Iraq in March 2003 had a negative impact on the then ongoing dialogue regarding political and economic reforms. After 2004, no further attempts were made to draft an economic reform program. Instead, the government concentrated on what could practically be achieved without having to formulate the reform tendencies into a document. In 2005, despite the convening of the 10th national conference of the Baath party, the reform dialogue was not resumed and the government replaced further discussion of economic reforms with the issuing of the 10th Five Year Plan (2006-2010) as a key instrument to guide the economy. This was a sort of returning to old rules of planning from above; and even if the FYP included specific discussions regarding the reform program, it had no practical value for the implementation of reform.

The struggle over economic reform

While the Syrian government meant to contain any political struggle over economic reforms, this struggle seemed too strong to stifle and had already acquired deep roots. Economic reform is a controversial issue governed by two sets of contradictions. The first are contradictions of a more technical and non-contentious nature, which occur as a result of difficult choices coupled with the difficulty and fear of change. These contradictions emanate from differences in viewpoints among business people, leaders of governmental economic departments and economic researchers over the most efficient means of stimulating socio-economic development. The second set of contradictions lies in contentious political tendencies, emanating from conflicting interests since any reform program is a representation of class, group or personal interests, which contradict and oppose other interests. In this sense, adopting a market economy is more than a technical position in the interest of greater efficiency or raising productivity. It is rather a social decision involving conflict between powerful interests. That conflict is not only about a choice between centralized economy and market economy, but also about what type of market economy and about the roles and interests of different groups or people within this market economy. Reform is economic in scope and social in results, and above all it is a political decision par excellence. Economic reform in Syria has been trapped between pressures exerted by two major different forces: one pushing towards reform and the other raising obstacles in front of it.

Forces pushing towards reform

The disintegration of the former socialist camp deprived the Syrian economy of a major source of support. This paved the way to shift from the statist economic system. This economic system went into crisis because the partial reforms of the mid 1980s proved ineffective. When economic recession reappeared in the second half of the 1990s it became evident to the Syrian leadership that maintaining the former economic system was likely to yield more harm than good and that change was inevitable.

Another factor was expanding globalization--the progress of free market economies worldwide, and greater interaction between national economies and international markets, with higher importance assigned to export and investment promotion. This has been pressuring the Syrian economy to shift to a market economy and acquire its legislative, regulatory and institutional infrastructures.

Syria's foreign economic relations also constitute a considerable source of pressure towards a market economy. The Great Arab Free Trade Agreement (GAFTA) agreement, the negotiations on a Syrian-European association agreement, widening economic and commercial relations, relations with international organizations and even diplomatic relations are generating constant pressures on policy-makers to move faster towards the realization of a market economy. A conviction evolved that a market economy and expanding the role of the private sector would ultimately contribute to improving Syria's relations with western European countries, which have fluctuated between cold, strained and tense on various occasions.

Facilitating the move toward the market was the fact that Syria had maintained, even under statism, a relatively strong private sector. After the agrarian reform measures and nationalization of industries in the 1960s, followed by expansion of the public sector in the 1970s, no further measures were taken towards reducing the private sector role. Public sector expansion ceased after the mid 1980s while the private industrial sector grew since the 1970s.

Over the past decades, a private business class steadily gained momentum. The 1980s crisis and the socialist collapse was an occasion for this class to expand its activity and increase its power on the ground. A major part of the Syrian business community grew under government patronage and care. Another part was founded by the children of government officials and institutional leaders, and had therefore enjoyed special privileges and influence. The growth of this business group created a lobbying interest advocating the market economy.

Forces opposing reform

The new circumstances and emerging forces created a powerful driving force towards economic reform. At the same time, the Syrian leadership is facing a number of difficulties and challenges in its reform effort. Most important among the obstalces to reform are the following:

The Baath party institutionalized its etatist-populist ideology. Pursuant to the Constitution, Syria is "a socialist popular democratic state" (article 1, clause 1), and "the economy of the state is a planned socialist economy aimed at eliminating all forms of exploitation" (article 13, clause 1). In addition to the ideological implications of this orientation, the overall policies, developed since 1963 till 2000, and particularly after 1966, were designed to serve the alliance on which the Baath authority was built, embracing workers, farmers, low-incomers and revolutionary intellectuals under army leadership, and against "exploiting capital." The Baath party came to power through such ideological discourse and alliance, and it is not easy to change that ideology while keeping the same ruling groups in power. If the ruling authority said it was heading for a market economy and granting the private sector a leading role, with all the resulting policies and measures, it then would have to answer questions as to why it gave up the leading role of the public sector and social protection and what social implications would result from the new trend. These questions touch the very core of the historical alliance on which Baath power was based.

Second, the hierarchal structure of the Baath state created a formidable obstacle to reform. The regime consisted of a number of overlapping hierarchical structures which yielded moral and material benefits for those assuming key positions within them. The leadership on top of the pyramid controls the state administrative apparatus through political organizations at the center, the regional level and the village level. These include the Baath party, the Federation of Workers' Unions, the Youth Union, the Farmers' Union, women's and students associations, as well as the professional and scientific federations. Changing this system is likely to threaten the interests of those controlling these structures. What is even more important here is that no matter how powerful the Syrian Presidency is, it would still need this large network as a tool to maintain a firm grip on power. Loosing the support of these groups could undermine stability at a time when Syria is facing ongoing threats.

Third, economic liberalization would considerably reduce the role of the public sector, thus depriving the state of its pivotal role, and turning it into an employer of a smaller number of workers that produce less commodities and services, thus lowering the number of those with interests linked to the state. The state would lose a tool that played a vital role during economic and political crises and create fears of an uncontrollable capitalist economy. Reform is also facing opposition from the government bureaucracy that produced a bureaucratic bourgeoisie which amassed huge wealth and whose interests would be threatened by change. Although these persons often have turned into businessmen with an interest in opening the door for the private sector, they cannot afford to relinquish the use of the state apparatus as a tool to generate profits since they lack the qualifications to compete on a market free of state intervention.

Reform is also facing opposition from the private sector which had emerged and developed under high protection against competition, creating an environment for lucrative gains at the expense of quality and consumer interests. Therefore, conservative and reform-opposing forces are not limited to the government and public sector; they exist in the private sector as well.

Public fear of reform, which is linked in people's minds to threats to already low living standards, and fear that the promised prosperity may never come, or only after years of deprivation and impoverishment, creates public anti-reform pressure. For example, there is a widespread fear of lifting the government subsidy for heating fuel (sold at SYP 7 = ca. 14 cents per liter), which explains the government reluctance over many years to take this decision. The government is afraid that reform could damage its public image, that it would be seen as betraying the poor to serve the rich, which is likely to expose larger groups of people to opposition discourses, particularly those of the Salafi groups in a country overwhelmed by an undeclared but obvious wave of religiosity. It is apparent that religiosity often places individuals at the threshold of extremism, especially in international circumstances plagued with double standards that inflame Muslims and persuade them of the 'obligation of Jihad'.

There is also the threat of corruption which gives rise to the claim that the reform recipe is designed to serve the narrow personal interests of a parasitic bureaucratic bourgeoisie. Small groups close to the decision-making circles have started to dominate wider areas of the most important and profitable sectors. This creates extensive complaints in the business community.

The long distance Syria needs to travel in order to shift from the status quo towards a market economy creates additional difficulties due to the discrepancy between the adopted new mechanisms and the prevailing system. There is a contradiction between the centralized structure of the Syrian economy on one hand and capitalist market mechanisms on the other, making changes a formidable challenge and consequently the threats of failure much greater. This is exacerbated by the lack of experience with regard to market mechanisms: the lack of local experts in market legislative and organizational structure who are capable of regulating the financial market, banking systems, free trade and shifting towards currency convertibility; the lack of sound knowledge on how to properly deal with transnational corporations and financial and trade institutions; inefficient marketing methods; underdeveloped business support institutions like research and consultancy centers, accounting and auditing firms and others; and, finally, the lack of reform leaders and cadres that could mobilize community forces behind the reform process.

Finally, and by contrast to eastern European countries, which received tremendous support from Western Europe, Syria is undertaking the reform without international support. Furthermore, it is doing so under external threats and pressure which leaves the government more vulnerable to the negative consequences of this process. It also makes it more reluctant to abandon its control over the national economy and the business community. This translates to the government's slow and selective pursuing of reforms which makes it harder to sustain a proper balance between change and stability.

The Syrian government's reform strategy

The difficult position of Syria and the conflict between pro and anti-market forces has made the Syrian leadership's reform path appear confused, but it has made up its mind to proceed toward a market economy, without declaring this explicitly. It refrained from formulating a specific and written reform program in order to avoid opposition and paying the legitimacy costs among its historic constituency. Also, avoiding an explicit declaration of its plans gives it more flexibility in dealing with reform supporters and opponents. Its strategy was to incite discussion of reform without adopting a specific stand in order to gradually prepare attitudes to accept reform inside state and party circles. The government would take steady, incremental steps towards building a market economy, gradually allowing the private sector to take the initiative. Practically, there is an unwritten and undeclared reform program, which is materializing into a legislative and regulatory framework for a market economy. Five years after taking several early steps towards a market economy, the ruling Baath party openly said it would adopt "social market economy" during its 10th conference in June 2005. The Syrian government viewed this formula as consistent with the social roots of the Ba'th party as it had evolved toward a combination of the market and encouragement of private investment, but with social protection for the poor or victims of reform. Other than this no party authority has so far prepared any document on the practical implications of a social market economy. Meanwhile, steps towards economic liberalization and building a liberal market economy continue unabated associated with a retreat of the state and the social insurance network.

The implementation of reform

In spite of the absence of a clear roadmap, Syria has made considerable strides towards completing various aspects of the market economy legislative, regulatory and institutional framework.

Investment environment: Private investment promotion has been among the first tangible government measures since the mid-1980s. That approach initially tried to attract private investment through tax and other incentives but did not create a comprehensive investment-friendly environment. The first investment promotion legislations was Decision 186, of 1985, by the Supreme Council for Tourism encouraging tourist investment and implementing many related projects. Legislative Decree 10 of 1986 provided an incentive for private and joint agricultural investments. A number of joint-ventures were set up under this law, but yielded insignificant results. Then Law 10 of 1991 offered tax and tariff exemptions as well as trade and exchange transaction facilitation. Many projects were authorized under this law, which covered the transport and industry sectors. Recently, Law 8 of 2007 replaced Law 10 of 1991, and Decree 9 of 2007 created the Syrian Investment Commission. The new investment law reduced the tax ceiling from 36% to 27% and replaced the tax holiday of 5-7 years with a so-called "dynamic tax reduction," depending on the legal form of the company, the number of employees, the region of investment, exports from the investment and others factors. All commodity and service sectors have been opened to Syrian and non-Syrian capital since the investment legislation does not discriminate between Syrian and non-Syria investors. On the other hand, the public sector has remained frozen and has not been privatized.

Foreign Trade: The trade sector was the second to undergo early reforms with an easing of the government's control of trade. The state gave up its monopoly on imports of several commodities, leaving them entirely for the private sector or authorizing the private sector to import certain goods in return for a 2-4% commission, including cars, iron and timber. It also lifted absolute bans on import of a large number of items similar to locally produced subsidized goods, but continued high customs duties.[1] Generally speaking, however, customs duties were reduced, especially in regard to production inputs, which went down to 1%.

A major watershed was Syria's signing of GAFTA in 1997, which opened Syrian markets to Arab manufactured products for the first time in decades. Syria also signed bilateral free trade agreements with the UAE in

2000, Saudi Arabia in 2001, Iraq in 2001, and Jordan in 2002, in addition to similar agreements previously signed with Libya, Egypt and other countries. A free trade agreement concluded with Turkey came into effect in the beginning of 2007. Moreover, the government initialled a Euro-Mediterranean Association Agreement, although this was not finalized due to French opposition and US pressure. Syria also applied for WTO membership in 2001, but its request was not considered owing to US opposition. Despite that the Syrian Prime Minister issued Decision 1006 of 2006 which set up a committee to prepare for WTO accession.

However, the foreign trade sector remained *de facto* closed to non-Syrian investments. Although there are no clear instructions prohibiting the establishment of import/export companies with non-Syrian capital, no such companies have been approved. Instead, natural and legal persons were allowed to act as agents for foreign companies, following a two and a half years ban on such a practice which, in any case, had been ineffective since foreign companies enlisted the assistance of undeclared agents which deprived the state coffers of revenues generated by such dealings. Syria joined a number of international agreements on protection of authorship and industrial intellectual property rights, patents, protection of technical and literary systems and international trademark registration.

Foreign trade liberalization measures constituted an opportunity to expand private sector trade activity, in that it opened the Syrian markets for imports and represented a gradual reduction in tariff protection of the industrial sector. It did improve the investment climate. However, trade liberalization in recent years became a matter of controversy, reflective of the struggle between manufacturers and traders, and between consumer interests (although trade liberalization has actually raised prices) and workers who wish to preserve their jobs threatened by imports.

Internal trade: Despite statist policy since the mid-1960s, government involvement in internal trade remained limited compared to the role of the private sector. It was limited to monopolies of certain 'strategic' commodities, notably oil products, cereals, cotton, iron, timber, cars and machinery. State-run cooperatives were set up for retail trading, but they had a small market share. However, the state began to gradually give up that role. More of a problem for traders was the issue of price controls which were based on profit margins. Government regulation of prices and its supply-monitoring has, however, eased since the mid-1990s. Law 42 of 2006 on protecting the national economy from practices harmful to trade was issued to protect Syrian industry from unfair practices in international trade, such as dumping and subsidies. Internal trade, particularly retail trading continued to be controlled by small and micro enterprises. No big companies or supermarket chains emerged. Only recently shopping malls began to appear in major cities. Until recently, non-Syrian investors were not in practice allowed to set up internal trading companies in Syria, although the law of commerce did not explicitly prevent it, and none have so far appeared. Recently, a modernized Law of Commerce No. 33 of 2007 was issued and is expected to be followed by a corporate law, which will together replace the old Law 149 of 1949 and which explicitly authorizes non-Syrian trading companies. A consumer protection society was set up, but remained ineffective. The government has failed to effectively promote consumer cooperatives which suffer from bureaucratic interference.

Monetary policy: Syria was in the mid-1950s one of the first countries to establish a Central Bank and had an advanced monetary policy compared to the neighboring countries. However, the state started to dominate the monetary institutions and placed the Central Bank under direct guardianship since the early days of the Syrian-Egyptian unity (1958-61). By the early 1980s, the Central Bank and monetary policy were completely paralyzed. It gradually recovered since Law 23 of 2002 created the Monetary & Credit Council which granted the Central Bank a larger role in developing the country's monetary policy. The multiple Syrian pound exchange rates against foreign currencies were unified.

Foreign trade financing rules used to be very complicated, and very often caused additional costs for traders. At present these instructions have been streamlined to a very large extent. Payment facilities were also offered with regard to current accounts to cover foreign trading. The so-called "export proceeds" rule, under which hard currency had to be earned through exporting in order to be able to finance imports, was abolished. Syrians now are allowed to open hard currency accounts. Interest rates were reduced after 20 years of fixed interest rates. Law 24 of 2005 allowed the establishment of money exchange companies and 5 companies were licensed by the end of 2007. Law 15 of 2007 regulated micro finance institutions. These changes contributed to increasing the hard currency supply in the local market, which helped stabilize the Syrian currency's exchange rates.

The Banking industry: After four decades of a government monopoly on banking, the sector was liberated. Private Banks Law 28 of 2001 was issued, and the first three private banks were founded in early 2004. By the end of 2007, the number of private banks in Syria had reached eight (two of which are Islamic banks) with 52 branches around the country, in addition to a number of new applications still under consideration. Under Law 29 of 2001 all banks were subject to banking confidentiality; Law 33 of 2005 on combating money laundering and financing terrorism was also passed.

The private sector share of bank credits increased from 24% in 2000 to 50% in 2005. Banking services in general improved, and the private banking sector contributed to offsetting the government banks' inability to meet the needs of the Syrian economy for modern banking systems. However, the capital of private banks remained limited and these banks have not expanded their activities on a large scale. Thus, the role played by the public sector in the domain of banking services continues to be dominant but, due to its antiquated operations and lack of proper salaries and incentives, it is expected to decrease with the further development of the private sector. The banking industry has not yet reached international standards and its contribution to investment financing is also limited. More time will be needed for such services to be elevated to the needed standards.

The Insurance industry: Following four decades of nationalization and government monopoly on the insurance industry, Law 48 of 2004 created an Insurance Supervision Commission and Law 43 of 2005 allowed private insurance companies. 2005 witnessed the establishment of the first private insurance company and by the end of 2007 nine of them were operational. However, the insurance market in Syria is still limited, and insurance culture is underdeveloped. The state-run Syrian Insurance Company still possesses the lion's share of the insurance and insurance services market. Only after many years will an expanding insurance market be in operation. But by then, the Syrian Insurance Company will not be capable of competing with private insurance companies if it continues to operate without reforming work incentives.

The financial sector: Law 22 of 2005 created the Syrian Commission for Financial Markets and Securities and, likewise, Law 55 of 2006 established a stock exchange. This was followed by the Prime Ministerial Decision which regulates the transactions conducted by brokerage firms at the stock market, whose opening was delayed to 2008. The creation of the stock market is expected to improve the investment climate and provide better financing for development by expanding the ownership base. Establishing an effective stock market requires a number of still missing conditions, such as competent professionals to run the market, rewarding salaries, financial accounting, evaluation and brokerage companies, portfolio management as well as an effective and transparent judiciary that protects the rights of different parties and controls fraud and speculation that may harm smll investors. The new Law of Commerce as well as the long-awaited Corporate Law were issued in March 2008, legalizing several types of trading companies, including leasing companies. The number of stock companies in Syria is very small but these changes increased interest among private and family enterprises in changing into stock companies.

Taxation: A series of steps were taken to reform the taxation system as a whole. A sales tax was implemented and scores of other taxes belonging to past decades were abolished. Law 61 of 2004 regulated the sales tax on a relatively large number of commodities. Law 41 of 2007 created the general authority of taxes and duties to handle tax policy design and follow up implementation. However, the reform of tax administration has not yet improved labor skills, raised salaries and incentives, upgraded office equipment and introduced IT in order to promote efficiency and combat corruption. Despite the issuance of Law 25 of 2003 on the combating of tax evasion, this legislation has remained ineffective, because the government did not pursuit serious enforcement and the private sector vehemently opposed it. Furthermore, the tax reforms have encouraged investment but were socially unfair, favoring major investors without providing minor investors with incentives.

Efforts were also made to reform the tariff system and improve customs efficiency. Law 15 of 2001 exempted exports from taxes and duties. Export taxes were reduced twice within three years. Law 24 of 2003, Law 60 of 2004 and Law 51 of 2006 were passed, with customs rates equal to or less than those of neighboring countries. Efforts to improve customs collections failed to achieve substantial successes: tariff evasion is still widespread and estimated customs revenues in 2006 budget did not exceed SYP 300 million while given the amount of imports it should have reached SYP 500 billion.

Public Finance: No remarkable changes occurred in public finance. Oil revenues, though declining, continued to flow into the treasury. The share of corporate tax has not increased much as a result of tax reductions on one hand, and because of the widespread tax evasion practices on the other. Sales tax revenues increased, and state funds continued to subsidize some commodities, especially diesel oil fuel. The value of these subsidies is estimated at $2.5 billion (around 10% of GDP). However, budgetary deficit rates started to rise over the past two years, reaching about 4% of GDP. The 2003 budget was issued with an approximate deficit of 33% (SYP 600 billion expenditure vis-à-vis SYP 400 billion revenues). The government continued to borrow directly from the Central Bank and not through treasury bonds although Decree 60 of 2007 was issued to organize the issuance of treasury bonds and bills. Despite some technical improvements in budget development and treasury management, no radical changes were made especially with regard to implementing programs to enhance the efficiency of collection and expenditure. The budgeting process remained at the level of collection and expenditure of revenue without allowing fiscal policy to be used for macro-economic management.

Syria's indebtedness levels were reduced following the settlement of debts to Russia and other former socialist countries. The settlement of government obligations, including debt service, particularly to the World Bank also contributed to improving the situation. Foreign debt declined to 17.2% of GDP by the end of 2007 compared to 23.3% in 2005

Rental relationships: Four decades after the issuance of highly protective legislation regarding real estate and land tenancy that had negatively affected the construction industry and blocked major agricultural projects, Law 6 of 2001 on house rental and Law 56 of 2004 on agricultural relationships reduced protection for tenants and laid out new regulations to resolve old rental arrangements. Similar to lease legislation in many countries, favoring the strong (owners) at the expense of the weak (tenants), these laws have provided a favorable environment for large private investments in real-estate (both for housing and business purposes).

Labor market policies: The Syrian labor policy was characterized by 'overprotection' of workers after the issuance of Law 91 of 1959 and the state social employment policy since the 1960s. Syria has now adopted gradual labor market liberalization and signed a number of international agreements on labor legislation and child labor. It also created a small credit scheme under the 'Agency for Combating Unemployment' which was set up pursuant to Law 71 of 2001. It was followed by Decree 38 of 2006, which created the General Commission for Employment & Projects Development, to replace the ACU. In addition, a new labor law was drafted, which is expected to replace Law 91 of 1958, in order to improve labor market flexibility and enable employers to discharge employees upon payment of an indemnity. Labor unions, however, strongly opposed the new law and it was temporarily frozen but it is expected to be enacted in the end.

The new policy is characterized by lifting the worker 'over protection.' This encourages investment, but there is still a need to activate the unions' role in the private sector. The trade union movement is very weak in this sector; given high unemployment levels, workers will remain under the total control of their employers who will be able to lower wages and privileges. Worker registration in the social security programs includes only 18.9% of private sector workers and they are registered with minimal salaries while all public sector workers are registered in accordance with the regulations and with full salaries. Pensions and end-of-service compensations are low compared to deductions that reach up to 24% of the worker's salary. This creates a market imbalance in favor of employers, which the regulatory bodies are too weak to compensate for. Also, training and retraining programs aimed at promoting productivity are still limited.

Education: Since the 1960s, the state nationalized education on the grounds that education plays a major role in raising generations on the values of the revolution. Under reform, Decree 36 of 2001 allowed the private sector, both local and foreign, to invest in higher education. Today there are about 10 private universities, in addition to a number of applications for new ones under consideration. Pre-university education also witnessed large expansion in private schools (more than 500) providing quality education that excelled the public school level. A number of those private schools were affiliated with international educational institutions and adopted international curricula in addition to the obligatory Syrian syllabus. Those quality schools, being costly, were confined to children of wealthy people, and low income parents had no other alternative except sending their children to free public schools. This separation laid the foundation for social separation between quality education for the rich and lower quality for the poor. Some go further and call for reducing government expenditure on education and health. These changes threaten to sharply divide society into classes and reduce social mobility.

Media: Since the 1960s, the state nationalized the media because information plays a major role in shaping allegiances. Gradual openness of the media and information sector started as of 2001. Legislative Decree 50 of 2001 authorized publication of private weekly and monthly magazines and newspapers. At present, there are over 200 such publications in Syria, covering various subjects. Parties' newspapers were also allowed to be sold on the market. Political dailies were also allowed but have to follow convoluted methods of publication and distribution: the two authorized political dailies, namely *Al-Watan* and *Al-Balad*, are published in the Damascus free zone and require a daily distribution permit, just like foreign journals. Also, publication of those dailies was authorized to persons loyal to the ruling regime. Twelve commerical radio stations with no political inclinations were also allowed. Two private TV stations were launched in 2007 and the private media is expected to expand, but under self-censorship.

Advertising: with the nationalization of the media in the 1960s, advertising was also nationalized. Several advertising companies were issued permits to operate privately over the past years. These include advertising dailies, roadside advertising boards, specialized directories like Yellow Pages and Medical Pages etc. The advertising market is steadily expanding, although it is still lagging behind other countries in the region. The exhibitions industry has thrived since the mid-1990s. While previously the Damascus International Fair was the only annual event, held every year since 1955, today scores of private exhibition companies have emerged, and the private sector seems more interested in internal and foreign exhibitions. Advertisement activity constitutes a precondition for market and investment growth.

Real estate: Real estate rental laws have restrained the growth of this sector, which played a very limited role in the past years. It has now been considerably liberalized, especially when Gulf companies started a number of investment projects in Syria, such as the UAE construction company EMAAR and the Kuwait Kharai Company. Two Legislative Decrees (6 of 2001 & 10 of 2006) liberalized the rental relationship between lessors and lessees. For the first time, Syrian companies began to invest in real estate, which, in turn, expanded the local construction materials industry and its imported inputs, and contributed to economic growth. Real estate prices and land prices have started to rise.

Micro enterprises: Syria's traditional policy was to support small and micro enterprises by restricting larger enterprises. One such example is the restrictions on the creation of car transport companies, which led to the passenger and goods transport sector being run by tens of thousands of individual owners. Similarly, the absence of chain supermarkets or shopping malls resulted in tens of thousand of shop owners sharing retail trade. Now with the change of economic policy towards large investment, small enterprises will face greater competition. The Agency for Combating Unemployment and non-profit organizations now offer support to this sector. Also, the government aims to further develop the spirit of initiative among the young generation, urging them to create their own businesses, given that the Syrians have a history dating back thousands of years during which they excelled as businessmen and traders.

Privatization: Although Syria has not yet taken the privatization pathway, the public economic sector has not expanded since the mid-1980s. On the other hand, public-private partnerships (PPP) has been encouraged. The establishment of a paper mill in Deir Ezzor under a public-private partnership was a leading example. However, the private sector appears to be unenthusiastic about investing in the public sector. Furthermore, the government set up a number of committees for public sector reform, but failed to achieve any positive results. The attitude towards the public sector exemplifies the regime's position toward reform in general, preserving its populist constituency and maintaining an instrument to intervene in economic life while also building a market economy. Thus, it preserves a fragile public sector without seeking any reforms which would threaten vested interests in the administration and among certain capitalist elements that are parasitic on the public sector. This results in large losses to the treasury and foregone economic growth for the national economy, despite the fact that public sector reform is possible and only needs the political will.

Consequences of economic reforms

In the first seven years of President Bashar al-Assad's term in office, 416 Laws and 492 Legislative Decrees were issued, a majority of them concerning economic reform. This in itself is an indicator in the extent of change in the legislative and institutional framework. Notwithstanding the gap between legislative enactment and implementation, it is an indicator of coming big changes in Syria's political economy. Despite the immaturity of the Syrian economic reform and its relative slowness, and despite the long way Syria still has to go in order to build a confident market economy in terms of legislative, regulatory and institutional structures, and despite the slow accumulation of know-how, the reforms have started Syria on an irrevocable pathway towards a market economy. We can assess the positive results by comparing Syria's current situation with an assumed situation had the reforms not been started. In a time when oil production has been declining, growth rates would have been lower and unemployment levels higher; the value of the currency would have declined, and budget deficits and inflation increased. The changes are neither totally positive nor negative, however, and there are also many indicators of dangers ahead.

Improved economic performance

There has been a tangible improvement in the investment climate, and an increase in investment rates (25% of the GDP in 2006-08 compared to 17% in 2000-04). Moreover, more foreign investments have started to flow in, especially billions of dollars of Arab investment. EMAAR of the UAE announced a multi-billion investment project; other giant companies such as Bin Laden (Saudi Arabia), al-Khurafi (Kuwait) and al-Diyar (Qatar) have also started projects. Most investment from the Arab Gulf countires are in such real estate projects. This is the first time Syria experienced such an investment boom, largely as a result of the increase of oil prices. In 2007, Syria's share reached 9.9% of the total FDI in the Arab countries, as investments reached approximately $600 million in 2006 and $ 787 million in 2007, which is 6.5 times larger than in 2002. Syrian capital is starting to reinvest rather than export its profits, as was the case during the last four decades. This almost raised growth rates to double population growth, reaching 4.5% in 2005, 5.1% in 2006 and an estimated 6.5% in 2007 compared to 0% in 2000 and -2.5 in 1999. Syria's exports increased from $ 5.6 billion in 2000 to $10 billion in 2006 and then to $ 12.4 billion in 2007 despite the decrease in oil exports as increased oil prices compensated for decreased production. Imports reached $14 billion in 2007 and the trade deficit dropped to $500 million in 2006, which was compensated for by the money transfers from Syrians working abroad; however, the trade deficit increased to $1.7 billion in 2007 (SYP 693 billion imports against SYP 615 billion exports). Exports of traditional industries exceeded oil exports, after the latter had dominated exports for 15 years. Textile and garment exports increased to $3.5 billion, a significant indicator that Syria has alternatives to declining oil exports. As a result, unemployment levels dropped to 8.5% according to official statistics.[2] Manufacturing industry (especially textile, food and pharmaceuticals) along with tourism proved to be important sectors, while the continuous growth of the pharmaceutical industry's competitiveness and exports was particularly striking. The real estate sector, once small and lacking big operators, started to grow as several real estate companies were established with Syrian capital. This led to a boom in land prices, especially in Damascus, Aleppo and other governorate centers. The most important positive indicator of reform might be the improvement of the Syrian pound's exchange rate against the American dollar (by the end of 2007 1 $ = SYP 48 while it was SYP 52 in 2005). This indicates the high dollar market supply and the similarity between the official exchange rate and that of the black market. Foreign debt is low and Syria has high foreign reserves of over 60% of GDP. The balance of payments has at times been in surplus and the budget deficit is still manageable (the deficit without oil revenues is 10% compared to 15% with oil revenues in 2004). All this happened despite regional instability and American pressures.

Economic performance since reform can be located in the wider context of Syria's development since 1970. As the figure below indicates, Syria experienced two peaks of GDP growth, the first in the 1970s and the second in the first half of the nineties, both of which were partly owing to an influx of Arab financial aid and the expectation of a possible end to the war with Israel and improved relations with the West. The two troughs occurred in the 1980s and in the second half of the nineties when these positive factors disappeared. The reform period, 2000–2008 is divided between the first 5 years when the GDP growth rate was around 2%, less than population growth of 2.4%, and the period 2006–2008 when the average of GDP growth was around 5%.

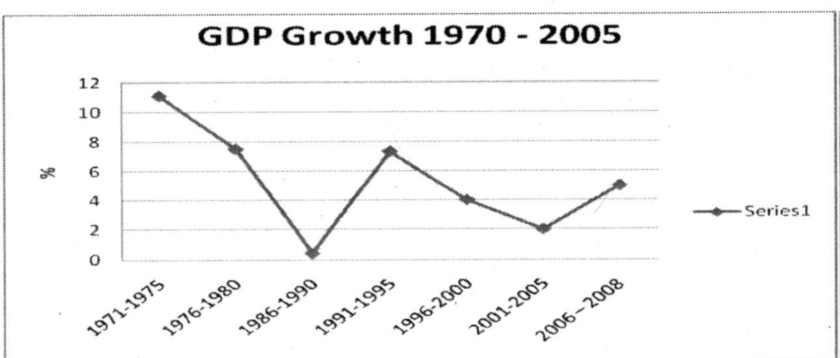

Private sector growth

Private companies have started to face greater competition pushing them to undertake self-restructuring, with a focus on modernizing their internal structure. This took the form of a wave of preparations to shift from family companies to joint stock companies and Decree 61 of 2007 was issued to facilitate this. Private companies also began to focus more on human resources and training, consultancy and improved auditing practices; they also started to prove their role in exports. In 2007, two large holding companies owned by Syrian businessmen, Alsham Holding Co. and Syria Holding Co., were established. Furthermore, the retail market has been modernized. Shops are now filled with a variety of goods, compared to the limited variety and low quality products that were available before the reforms. Shops now look better as compared to their hitherto shabby appearance and modern cafés and restaurants have sprung up. On the negative side, economic reform has focused on fiscal, financial and trade reform while industry and agiculture, which have been neglected, have suffered in the last few years.

Social Impact

The gap between rich and poor increased and social differences started to become more apparent after being hidden and limited. Society has started to divide into two main classes, one with access to better private education and healthcare, and better social welfare. Luxurious cars now cover the streets, and the rich have special markets separated from those where the poor shop. The second class consists of people that barely have access to public education and healthcare, or even to daily food. Richer people now brag about their wealth freely and the new generation is expressing its consumer wants freely despite pressures from salafi religiosity. The media and communication networks, especially TV and the Internet, are playing a crucial role in integrating Syria into the global society with both its negative and positive impacts.

Negative effects include price increases, which have started to damage the living standards of wider social categories; price rises have been absorbing all salary increases, despite the fact that state workers salaries have increased by 85% over five years (2001-2006) and subsequently affected the private sector salary levels. For instance, the price index increased by 10% in 2006 compared to 2005 according to the Central Bureau for Statistics, while salary levels remained unchanged. If we add housing costs to the goods and service basket of 2006, price increases will reach 17%, with those for 2007 even higher. The main reason behind these price increases is the international rise in the prices of oil, oil derivatives, petrochemical products and raw materials such as iron, timber, copper and aluminum as well as foodstuffs including wheat, barley and oils while wages and salaries remained the same in both the private and public sector during 2006 and 2007. Salary levels in both public and private sectors are not enough for a descent life for most workers.

The resentment of the poor could be clearly heard but in private since public demonstrations are banned in the country. The UNDP poverty report shows that in 2003-2004 around 2 million people (11% of the population) lacked access to basic food and nonfood requirements. Using another poverty line, the overall proportion of people in poverty was at 30%, including 5.3 million persons. If this survey had been conducted in 2008, poverty rates would have been higher still. In order to face this situation, the state is seeking to preserve some components of the previous social security network, but it failed to develop new techniques for preventing sharp social polarization. Syria used to have a social pyramid characterized by a wide base, a big middle stratum and a low peak; under economic reform, the middle strata are shrinking while a rich stratum is emerging at the top, resulting in a social pyramid with a broad base, a narrowing middle stratum and a higher peak.

Changing roles: government, private sector, and civil society

A clear change is being witnessed especially on the economic level as the private sector is becoming the major contributor to GDP, by 65% according to official figures and more than 70% according to some estimates. It is also becoming the major employer as approximately 75% of the labor force in Syria work in the private sector, which dominates most of the economic sectors. The role of the state economic sector is decreasing, suffering from increasing problems and manifest in shrinking state involvement in the economy. The political role of the private sector outside official frameworks is growing. Private sector influence is gradually extending to the education and information sectors, two major sectors in forming public opinion, social values and loyalty. Businessmen are sponsoring sport clubs that had been under government control since the 1970s due to the fact that they were places for public gathering. The private sector's ability to mobilize the forces of the civil society is rising after the degradation suffered by public secondary associations, with the result that society's primordial bonds like family, sect and religion have increased in saliency which has come to supercede loyalty to the country for many social categories. This change is reflected in the increased ability of capitalists and tribal leaders to get their representatives elected as members at the parliament and local administration councils; indeed, were these conducted on a transparent basis without state intervention their impact would be dominant.

What remains to be done?

It is difficult to answer this question because there is no ready-made blueprint for reform or for a market economy since it differs from country to country and the government has not laid down clear targets. However, it is clear that Syria still has a very long way to go during the next years to reach its formal goal of a "social market economy." One can identify general economic objectives, such as increased competitiveness on international markets, higher productivity, and value added, all of which are at a low level in Syria, and indicate legislative, regulatory and institutional reforms needed to advance these objectives. We will introduce here the main issues that the economic reform program is still to tackle.

Decision-making and implementation

Economic decision-making is a cornerstone of any reform process but it is still facing a twofold problem. In its technical aspect, decision-making still lacks competence, regular procedures and quality information. There is also a need to draw a roadmap specifying the reform steps, timing and requirements. In its political aspect the Baath Party is still controlling not only strategic decisions but intervenes in the smallest detail such as appointing a manager in a remote department. It is crucially important to activate community monitoring in different forms to guarantee that the reform process is on the right track and serves the public interest rather than vested interests which are increasingly shaping the reform agenda. No significant progress has been made in administrative reform despite the creation of a new portfolio, Ministry of State for Administrative Development in March 2000, which remains without a structure or resources. In the next cabinet, its importance decreased instead of increasing. The government has taken several steps to ease centralization and delegate authority to governors and local bodies, simplify procedures and focus on training and selection methods but this has yielded no tangible improvement in government efficiency. The judicial system also needs reform, for a market economy cannot be built without a mechanism to ensure rule of law and contract enforcement.

Combating corruption

Individuals and investors are still complaining about pervasive corruption. Transparency International's corruption index shows that corruption indicators in Syria actually deteriorated (see table 1.1). As Syria's global ranking indicates, in 2003-2004 Syria was around the world average, while in 2005 and 2006 its ranking fell.

Table 1.1: Transparency International Corruption Index: Syria 2003 - 2005

Total Score	Confidence Range	CPI Score	Country rank	Year
163	3	2.9	93	2006
158	3	2.9	93	2005
145	2.8	3.4	71	2004
133	1.3	3.4	69	2003

Combating corruption is one of the most important economic, social and political issues. It represents a condition for raising administrative efficiency and creating an attractive investment climate as well as for the best use of national wealth, political legitimacy and political reputation. A comprehensive program for combating corruption that involves all social categories is still to be initiated.

The private sector and the investment climate

The private sector has enjoyed protection from one side and suffered from many pressures from the other, as many private firms' characteristics do not go well with open markets. Private businesses are dominated by small, family enterprises that lack modern corporate structure and work methods; they do not disclose their information. High protectionism has ensured them guaranteed profits with almost no competition while open markets require competitiveness; over-regulation and pervasive corruption within the government bureaucracy have made this sector used to corrupt activities. Furthermore, business services still require much development. Management consulting is still at its primary stages, and so are auditing services. Moreover, the introduction and application of international accounting standards and disclosure practices are still very weak; the production of sufficient, comprehensive and timely information still needs much effort; and their internet services are still inefficient and plagued with troubles. Some private companies have become aware of this situation and began taking action in the right direction, but this is not a wide, well-coordinated movement within a comprehensive private sector reform program. This would be the task of the government and other private sector agencies such as the chambers of commerce and industry. Here it is especially important to launch an industrial modernization program because industry is the sector facing the hardest competition as Syria moves toward a market economy.

The World Bank study on investment climate in Syria, conducted in 2005, indicates that the investment climate in Syria is still suffering from many weaknesses that limit investment attractiveness and product competitiveness.[3] The report was based on a field survey that included 448 small firms with less than 50 workers, 81 intermediate facilities with 51 – 150 workers and 25 large facilities with more than 150 workers. Main conclusions of the study were that, while Syrians' business initiative and talents were highly evaluated, electricity supply, corruption, business licenses and unfair competition issues constituted, according to 40% of the surveyed companies, strong or even severe obstacles to investment. Problems noted with the administration included the unpredictability of taxes that might be imposed by the tax administration, and over-regulation, with businesses subjected to around 25 inspections by municipality, police, social security and tax officers who often extract bribes and consume time and energy of the management. Syria has the slowest judiciary in the region: only 1% of the surveyed respondents had resolved their commercial conflicts in courts over the last 3 years. Bureaucratic procedures for initiating businesses were highly complex and investor protection low.

Another set of problems is related to labor. Workers' low productivity makes labor costs higher compared to output than in many countries; Syrian workers' education level is considerably lower than in other countries and the worker discharge difficulty indicator is higher than the average rate of MENA. The Ministry of Social Affairs and Labor drafted a new law to replace Law 90 of 1959, known for its inflexibility as regards the employer's right to discharge employees, which would give the employer the right to dismiss the worker in return for compensation up to threefold the monthly salary for each service year. However, this law faced fierce opposition from the Workers' Unions, delaying its issuance. In agriculture, land reform legislation still stipulates low limits for agricultural property, leading to the absence of developed capitalist agriculture, and to the fragmentation of land property among a great number of small farmers.

Another set of problems concern financing. Relatively few Syrian companies - only 12% of the surveyed companies - received financing from banks. Banks provided only 12% of the working capital and 4% of the total investment to the companies in the study. The average required collateral demanded by banks came to 217% of the loan value, one of the highest measured in ICA surveys. The monetary sector is still lacking the long-awaited stock market, investment guarantee institutions, financial services establishments, and the full convertibility of the Syrian pound. Moreover, capital inflows/outflows are still restricted; investment banks are absent; the payment system is still very inefficient with cash payment covering 90% of the private sector transactions; the informal private sector is estimated to be handling around 40% of market transactions; credit/debit cards are still absent and public banks services are still backward; the Central Bank's ability to supervise other banks is limited; and capital leasing firms are still absent in the country.

The United Nations Industrial Development Organization (UNIDO) indicated that Syria's economy is behind a number of economies in the region such as Egypt, Jordan and Tunisia. The minimum amount of required capital to form a company is six times more than the regional average. As regards investment promotion activity, the investment development agency lacks a plan to direct investments towards the most important sectors; provides insufficient information for the investor to decide on investment feasibility; and lacks sufficient promotion and marketing to attract investors.

Public sector reform

Syria has not chosen the privatization option and the government is still calling for public sector reform. However, despite the creation of several committees since 2001, no step has been taken in this regard, and the public sector is still suffering major losses when subsidies for oil products are deducted from profits. Even if the government wants to maintain its interventionary role in investment and job creation, this requires a public sector working with financial and administrative autonomy in coherence with market mechanisms. It also requires selecting specific investment sectors with strategic importance where the public sector can efficiently compete and withdrawing from other sectors to enable the private sector to compete in an open market. At present, the state monopolizes the manufacturing industry in fields such as tobacco, beer, mineral water and electricity distribution as well as trade in certain products such as oil derivatives, wheat, cotton and sugar beet. It intervenes in the trade of other products such as iron, wood and cars and imposes a 2-42% commission for allowing merchants to import such items without providing any services.

Conclusion

Syria has taken impressive, probably irreversible, strides toward a market economy; indeed the political struggle for reform appears to have been won. But Syria has still a long way to go before its reforms are fully implemented and a healthy market economy is in operation. Moreover, it is by no means certain that the ideal of creating a *social* market economy will be realized, for there are indeed signs that the outcome will be little different from the kind of unregulated capitalism prescribed by neo-liberalism. The following essay takes up this question.

---

[1] Many importers resorted to fraudulent practices to evade customs duty, such as tampering with the value included in the invoices of imported goods, or importing these goods via an Arab country with an Arab certificate of origin, or even cross-border smuggling.

[2] Economic experts are sceptical about this percentage for several reasons: the unemployment rate was 16% in 2003 according to a sample survey conducted by the Agency for Combating Unemployment; the rates of new entrants into the labor market is still high; the Syrian Government has lowered employment in the public sector; and around 200,000 to 300,000 workers returned to Syria from Lebanon in 2005.

[3] World Bank: "Syrian Investment Climate Assessment. Unlocking potential of the private sector," June 8, 2005.

2
A Model for a Social Market Economy in Syria

Introduction

Even as Syria seeks to move toward a market economy, the capitalist world economy has entered a deep structural crisis the costs of which the public, in the first place, has paid and will pay. The domination of the extreme neo-liberal ideology generated an unprecedented liberalization of the world financial markets. Speculative rent-based activities increased at the expense of the real economy (production of goods and services). The role of the state regressed and its regulation of markets loosened, resulting in a "thin" state which was, more than ever before, a tool in the hands of the business community; presidents became business promoters and transaction marketers. The social aspect declined and laborers lost many of the privileges that they had gained over long decades of struggling. Since the world economy depends on the dollar and other hard currencies, the business practices and crises in the core capitalist economies, especially the US, affect the whole world. As the USA issues more banknotes to cover its budget deficit, the entire world will pay for it. Nobody yet knows how far the rules of the world economy will change as a result of the crisis; there is no alternative to capitalism but neo-liberalism may retreat and newer state-centric economic models, such as that of China, become more attractive. Hence, just as the Syrian government seemingly opted for a market economy, this model has become more contentious, and alternative mixed models enjoy more credibility. The question is whether Syria can steer an economic reform path to a social market economy that enjoys the benefits of a market while avoiding the costs of an unregulated neo-liberal one.

Syria in the context of economic debates

The Syrian dilemma

For about 35 years, Syria followed economic polices modeled on the Soviet experience, but after the collapse of the Eastern Bloc, the Syrian government started hesitatingly moving towards the market economy. This hesitation reflected a conflict between its advocates and opponents and fear of the consequences of uncontrolled market mechanisms. Thus, in 2000, when President Bashar al-Assad took power, Syria adopted a slow experimental approach of change without formulating this approach in any document. The 10th Conference of the Arab Baath Socialist Party (June, 2005) officially adopted the Social Market Economy that in principle combines a market with social protections. But the party did not issue any document to explain the content of this model and Syria started transition from a state-run economy to a market economy without any methodology or guidelines measuring success or failure, nor mechanisms to take corrective actions.

This gave rise to different opinions about this choice. Some believed that a social market economy would not work because it needs a rich country (like Germany) to bear the costs. Others supported the new approach but called for staged implementation: first introducing a market economy in order to achieve growth and then the social aspects once growth had been achieved. The documents of the State Planning Commission seem to advocate such a market-first vision. A third party called for simultaneously combining the market with social aspects and a fourth party looked at this approach as a mere continuation of the old Ba'thist statist-populist model in new attire. The common point running through the debate was the ambiguity of the meaning of the social market model.

Meanwhile, in practice, step-by-step transition has already started toward a liberal market economy, and while the slow pace of transition may have concealed the impact on social welfare so far, this is bound to be negatively affected. The transition towards a market economy has achieved some positive results including increased investment and higher economic growth rates, but its socioeconomic effects have also started to appear, especially the negative impact on industry where once exporting industrialists have become importers, while the increased costs of living and deteriorating living standards of most Syrians has aggravated poverty. The poverty report on Syria issued by the UNDP states that "at the national level, well-off individuals (above the third tenth of expenditure distribution) have benefited from the economic growth more than the poor have" and that poverty "in general exists in rural areas (62%) more than in urban areas".

The UNDP reports also show that Syria's index of social development is declining, especially since the late 1990s. The increasing poverty and declining social index despite economic growth is reflected in the widening wealth distribution gap: the Gini index of inequality has increased in Syria between 1997 and 2004 from 0.33 to 0.37.

This is unjust from the perspective of socioeconomic democracy, and most Syrians will not accept an economic system that causes deterioration in their standards of living while a small minority owns the majority of the nation's wealth. Moreover, such a model would not be sustainable and would lead to increasing crime and social unrest. Efforts to avoid confronting social problems do not serve the cause of real economic growth.

The origins of the social market idea

Though the economic model to be proposed in this study is labeled a "social market economy" it does not only take the original German social market economy as its reference but benefits from the experiences of both Western and Eastern Europe, as well as Third World countries. It also takes the Syrian reality into account on the grounds that the economic model in any country is drawn to fit the socioeconomic geography of the country.

There are three essential reasons for not wholly adopting the German model as a reference: First, it is no more than an organized liberal market economy, based, as Dr. Issam Azzam said,[1] on "a difficult compromise that was realized in historically [specific] circumstances…in which… capitalism…[had to] to make significant cessions to the working class ….establishing a socioeconomic contract between laborers and employers under the state's supervision…[permitted by] the high level of economic development, which allowed dividing the economic surplus between the laborers and the employers; …and aimed at avoiding the threat of communism…which meant adopting platforms that took many things from communism." However, this model has been regressing in Western Europe since the liberal attack on the "welfare state" and with the collapse of the international socialist system, the capital countries have needed to pay less attention to social issues, notably equality. Also, the USA, working to impose its economic hegemony through opening of markets and unleashing competition, obliged the social market countries to diminish social security networks and the welfare state in order to reduce costs and increase their competitiveness, making it difficult for a single country to impose high taxes that would affect its competitiveness in an open market. This situation lessens the applicability of the previous forms of the social market economy. Moreover, the German European model has not paid attention to the central social issue in any socioeconomic structure, namely the "ownership of the means of production". It has not included the principle of expanding the basis of property ownership, or developing the role of participatory social property forms, and has been limited, basically, to the concept of concentrated corporate capitalist property which does not benefit most people in any given society. "Expanding the basis of property" does not mean expanding state property but rather the basis of individual ownership, even if in small properties. The number of owners and the property hierarchy are major criteria of social equity in any society (How many owners are there? How much do they own out of the total property values? And how are the categories of owners distributed?). While it is true that the German model has given good results in Germany due to high productivity and economic growth, this is not the situation in the developing countries including Syria where the ability to assume the costs of traditional forms of the social market economy is declining in today's open economy.

The debate over economic production and income distribution

The discussion of a social market economy provoked a lot of debate because social expenditure is a direct deduction from the national income (in Germany about 27% of the GDP is spent on social aspects). Neo-liberals argue that a deduction for social purposes that exceeds the capability of the economy will be at the expense of productive investment; this will weaken future growth, hence negatively affecting future investment and social expenditure. Conversely, they argue, maximizing investment will propel growth and increase the total of social expenditure, even if its proportion of national income remains limited, if not in the short term, over the long term. For neo-liberals, the social aspect is a byproduct and priority should be given to motivating investment, individual initiative and profits. This argument has its resonance in Syria, not only within the business community, but among governmental decision-makers[2] as well, who accept that social expenditure overburdens growth and drives investment away, and that we should postpone it in order to give private investment the opportunity to flourish freely without constraints. Only by realizing growth and enlarging the cake can one allocate a higher ratio for social expenditure. Moreover, for neo-liberals, a productive capitalist who reinvests his money to expand his/her business is much better than a government official who misuses his/her power to self enrich through corruption and wastes public money carelessly; the first realizes growth and benefit for others, while the second realizes his pleasures and causes harm to others.

Socialists, by contrast, argue for the importance of equitable social distribution from the fact that the economic growth of developed societies has been associated for many decades with a continuous improvement in the their wealth distribution and working conditions which, in turn, created a better climate for productivity to grow. Social expenditure is investment in human capital that contributes to health, education and qualifications needed for economic growth but market mechanisms alone limit this to richer groups and deprive the majority. Under a market economy, all contribute to income production, but productive property is monopolized by a few. Furthermore, producing goods and services is not an end by itself, but is to satisfy the needs of the people as a whole; postponing distribution traps the majority of people in poverty. If it is necessary to diminish consumption this should include everyone, not exempting the rich who consume wastefully. Finally, socialists would reject the argument that capitalists are necessarily productive and government necessarily parasitic.

The dictates of globalization

This theoretical debate has to be put in the current context, where international financial institutions, governments and economists tend to assume an inverse relation between the level of social protection and the competitiveness of open economies. Overcoming this contradiction and achieving both a high level of social protection and competitiveness is possible but it requires a high level of productivity and industries with higher added value, which allows for both higher wages and higher profits. This is the strength of the developed economies, which can do without low value-added sectors requiring intensive labor and focus on the sectors requiring intensive capital and high technology. Moreover, they also monopolize intellectual property rights and scientific research, thus putting high valued added industries out of the reach of the Third World countries, which allows them to impose high prices and profits of their products.

The world market with its flows of capital and goods limits the capacity of individual countries, especially small ones, to adopt policies that differ from the prevailing neo-liberal practices because this would isolate them. For example, it is not easy to apply a strong protection policy, or to adopt a restricted monetary system and impose high income taxes. On the other hand, adopting the neo-liberal model proved not to be the good choice, as the current crisis illustrates. However, when we get beyond the dominant discourses and closely analyze economic policies applied throughout the world we find that there are significant differences and other options are available. Based on that, we believe that the social market economy has sound foundations and principles and that they are applicable under the prevailing global conditions and can secure both economic growth and a fairer distribution of wealth for Syria.

Foundations of the model for a social market economy in Syria

Syria needs to formulate a clear strategy of its socioeconomic orientation and it should not let this be dictated by neo-liberal pressures. An effort is needed to formulate a model of the economy it aims for and the role of the state in this political economy. The model to be proposed here is not a mathematical model where the researcher enters the inputs to get certain results and to see the impacts of probabilities, assumptions, etc. Such models are merely an aid to analysis and are misused by some to claim absolute objectivity of analysis in order to exclude social aspects. Rather, the model entails laying out, on the basis of general principles, a strategy that would be able to realize balanced economic and social growth. The social market economy is based on the following principles.

The principle of the market economy

No economy today can exist outside of the market, but there is not one single model of a market economy in the past or at present. We believe that the social market economy should rest on the foundation of a market, which, in turn, stands on private property of the means of production, and freedom of entering and exiting the market, together with policies to enhance competition and combat monopoly. In addition, it needs a pricing mechanism based on supply/demand; it needs to develop initiative spirit, freedom of decision for economic institutions, and systems of values suitable for market economy.

At the same time, however, the market should not be left without government intervention, using soft administrative and financial tools, since a market without controls creates economic crises and wealth polarization, especially with the recently growing global trend to financial speculation. The social market economy is not a mere market economy, but is based on market forces that are controlled by effective political and social measures aiming at sustainable economic growth and better income distribution. It entails developing a set of policies that *work with* the principles of market economy, allowing market dynamics to stimulate economic growth. A social economy needs two legs to walk on: the first one is economic growth, which enlarges the cake, and the second is fair distribution. Only productivity will ensure success in the end. This is what we have learned from the collapsed socialist experience. Rigidity and failure to grow and keep up with the changes in the capitalist system brought collapse.

The social market model also focuses on integrating income distribution into the production process since this is not an automatic byproduct of the market. Thus, the model entails fair *wage policies and income re-distribution policies that correct market imbalances*. This model also depends on *expanding the basis of property* to include the broadest sector of people through individual private properties, collective private properties (collectives, associations or groups), small and medium enterprises (SMEs), and non-monopolistic stock companies. This model does not expand state property, but keeps it to the necessary minimum. This has nothing to do with the totalitarian state which monopolizes the economic activities and prevents, or hinders, individual and collective initiatives. But it does depend on a limited interventional role by the state through the legislation of a regulatory structure. Thus, all policies should have these two sides, and should hinder neither growth and production nor equity of income distribution.

The principle of the "smart state"

The need to redefine the role of the state is an urgent issue in Syria. All societies have to find a proper role for the state and for Syria neither an excessively totalitarian model nor the excessively weak neo-liberal state, nor one captured by narrow special interests are appropriate. A proper role for the state and especially its control of society is not easily devised: excessively tight controls suffocate society, excessively loose ones could lead to anarchy, but up to this point, control in Syria remains too strong and more freedom is needed.

Since independence, the Syrian state adopted a relatively high level of economic intervention. It followed a policy of protective tariffs to encourage national industry. With the Syrian-Egyptian Unity, the state started to play a central role in the economic, political and social life, a role which was strengthened after 1963. The state assumed direct control over a major part of the economic activity and production and had a great influence on the rest by its excessive interference in economic activity. It restricted private investment, monopolized investment of many sectors and controlled media and advertisement. It undertook provision of many free services such as education and health, and some commodities and services were delivered at subsidized prices such as bread, tea, rice, sugar, electricity, water and fuels. It imposed exorbitant tax rates on profits. By and large, it had direct control on a huge part of income and income distribution, following policies that aimed at income redistribution,

Today, the State is radically changing its economic role; the public sector has been frozen; investment liberalized; the market opened for local and foreign investment; trade liberalized, and many state-monopolies given up, such as foreign trade, banking, insurance, media and advertisement which have been liberalized; and the rental relation between owners and tenants in the real estate sector and in agricultural lands modified. The state is gradually relinquishing its price subsidization policy. It is reducing taxes by transferring the tax burden from the producer to the consumer/citizen.

This transformation is taking place piecemeal and covertly without debating a new definition of the role of the state, leading to the de facto assumption of the neo-liberal idea of the state's role by default, with hugely negative consequences for social equity and the development process as a whole. The liberal model represents the Anglo-Saxon model of capitalism, which is not the suitable model for a state like Syria for many reasons; rather, the model of the intervening state within the market economy remains the most suitable one for Syria. Liberals claim that market economy policies are neutral and of technical rather than social nature but we believe that the liberal market is socially not only unfair, but extremely unfair; it leads to the accumulation of wealth in few hands and to monopoly. Therefore, selective state intervention which does not contradict the general principles of market economy becomes a necessity; as an example, it is known that the absolute freedom of competitiveness leads to monopoly; therefore, all countries set legislation to protect competition and prevent monopoly. For the role of the state to be effective, it should be "smart" and include the following main aspects:

1. The role of the state as an organizer i.e. to create the legal, organizational and institutional environment for economic activity, including its intervention to correct market deviations and socioeconomic malfunctions using monetary, financial and commercial tools. This includes planning to create an investment promoting environment and an effective policy to support industry and develop technology.

2. The state's role as a arbiter among society's classes and groups to keep the social balance and correct social deformations created by the market, including preventing property and wealth polarization, encouraging the expansion of the property basis and income distribution through e.g. progressive taxation, social security and encouragement of trade unions.

3. Its role as a complementary investor: while the main body of the economy is in the hand of an individual and collective private sector, the state would still make strategic investments that the private/civil sector refrain from, invest in neglected sectors or regions, and correct supply/demand imbalances. Thus, it would enhance competition and prevent monopoly, but according to uniform principles and rules without privileging some. This role might take the form of pure government companies or joint ventures with the private sector. These state investments should be run not by the Ministry of Finance, but by (a) government holding company(ies) that operate(s) according to rules of market as it is the case all over the world (this is a call to reform the public sector not to privatize it).

4. The state's role is central in establishing the physical and social infrastructure for socioeconomic activity, which includes public utilities, roads, bridges, canals, dams, and other public facilities. In addition, this includes spending on education and health, which should be provided freely at all levels or with low fees for limited-income people, in order to prevent polarization in society.

The principle of fair macroeconomic policies:

Treasury policies regarding both revenues and expenditure differentially benefit social groups. Neo-liberal-inspired reforms in state policy are an immediate threat to the realization of a social market economy. In the past, Syria used to get a large part of its revenues from petroleum income which was redistributed for the good of a wide range of people in society, notably through subsidies. Today, petroleum income is declining and state income from its financial and commercial enterprises will also decline as the private sector acquires a growing part of this market. State income may also decline because of the reduction in tax rates on capital. Thus, the solution that may be adopted will be to abandon the policy of subsidies which would have a huge negative effect on the standards of living of a wide sector of citizens. Moreover, the Syrian government in the future could be forced to reduce further its education and health expenditures, which, if it happens, would have huge negative social impacts but also a negative effect on economic growth. This dilemma is the main direct threat to the whole idea of a social market economy and has to be addressed.

Tax policies have become an issue which risks determining by default Syria's model of development. Until 1992, punitive taxation on profits exceeding SYP 700,000 reached 92%, which became a pretext for tax evasion. Those rates have been reduced gradually until they reached now a minimum of 14% for stock companies that offer more than half of their stocks for public underwriting, and a maximum of 28%. This is very low by all international standards. Nevertheless, tax evasion is still very common and the contribution of direct taxes on real profits is still low. At the same time Syria is following neo-liberal practices which levy taxes on consumers rather than on profit making producers, that is to say, it is reducing the profit tax and replacing it partially by sales tax / VAT, and it decreases customs duties, which protect local products from imports.

Tax policy lacks a clear strategy and has to focus on combating tax evasion, particularly by large capital. It is incomprehensible that the government has not paralleled the drastic reduction in tax rates with increased combating of tax evasion including widespread customs evasion and smuggling. These practices deprive the treasury of significant resources, and would force the government to take further actions that hurt social equity.

Neo-liberal ideology shows a clear schizophrenic attitude to any price subsidization and protection. All evils are attributed to subsidies in the name of realizing a balanced budget; yet neo-liberal states themselves widely subsidize and protect their agriculture from foreign imports. Moreover, the pundits of liberalism have no effective solutions to the negative consequences of eliminating subsidies. In the past, Syria applied administrative pricing for socioeconomic development reasons, i.e. subsidizing education, health, culture and sport, as it is an investment in human capital to produce a qualified able-bodied labor force. For social and political reasons it also subsidized basic commodities like bread, rice, sugar, oil, electricity and fuels. There were economic reasons, too, for subsidizing energy and agriculture. And some subsidies benefited vulnerable people or those with special needs. Thus, the subsidization policy had multiple objectives and entirely relinquishing it is neither easy nor justified. Rather what is needed is an integrated strategy to diminish unnecessary or unjustified subsidies, while targeting continued subsidies more effectively. This would reduce waste while putting in place social safety nets.

The principle of expanding the productivity of the Syrian economy

Furthermore, a market requires establishing a regulatory and institutional structure and must be governed by macro-economic policies to foster growth. Designing and modeling such a policy should be based on field surveys assessing Syria's physical and human resources along with natural and technological resources. The policy should identify priority sectors that impact on growth in terms of increasing accumulation and strengthening the infrastructure of the Syrian economy, hence guaranteeing sustainable development. This means, first of all, developing a package of monetary, financial and commercial policies to encourage the development of these different sectors. Secondly, the establishment of a number of locomotive projects and programs that promote economic and social development such as technological parks and private economic zones hosting high-potential industries like the textile city, agrofood city, and software city, which aim at developing these industries and increasing their added value. These policies should be part of a long-term development program divided into three broad stages, each lasting a period of 7 years and preparing the ground for the following stage through expanding the production base horizontally (number of enterprises, investment volume, and number of employees) and vertically (value-added, capital-intensive and high-tech goods and services, and more a educated and trained workforce).

The preparation phase (7 years)
During this stage the focus should be on enhancing traditional industries (for example: food, textile, and assembly line industries, which may be the base for more sophisticated industries) as well as on tourism, transport and transit trade; education and training, and export of skilled labor to Arab oil countries. There should be integration between industries using local inputs and those using imported inputs as well as between those satisfying local demands and those intended for export. More advanced mechanical, electrical and chemical industries should occupy the second place while the third place should be for pioneer industries such as electronic and knowledge-based industries. Each industry should contribute to the general economic goals for this stage: realizing savings at more than 25% of GDP; reducing capital flight; investments levels exceeding 25% of GDP from local sources and FDI; an estimated growth rate of 6-7%; lowering the population growth rate from 2.5% to 2% and the unemployment rate below 10%; attaining a low budget deficit not exceeding 7%; and lower inflation rates below 10% by the end of the stage.

The launch phase (7 years):
In this phase more emphasis should be given to advanced goods and services with higher value-added, benefiting from the opportunities that will be available after the successful implementation of the first phase. Mechanical, electrical and chemical industries should become the core of Syrian industry in addition to improving services, such as insurance, finance, design, television programs, artistic performances and many other activities where the Syrians may excel. Traditional industrial sectors will maintain their importance in terms of absolute quality of production, export and added values. The development of pioneering industries such as electronic and communication industries will begin. The goals of this phase are to raise savings and investment by another 5%, and growth rates to 7-8% while lowering unemployment to around 7-8%.

Sustainable growth phase (7 years)
The main aim of this phase is to focus on knowledge-based, capital-intensive commodity and service industries that produce higher added value, such as electronic and communication industries, advanced financial, banking and insurance services, scientific researches and designs etc. Mechanical and electrical industries will keep the most important role in terms of size and value. Export industries services will receive greater care.

The main goals of this phase include raising investment to 35% of GDP, growth to 8-10% and lowering unemployment to 5%.

The principle of fair and productive wage and labor market policies

These policies are a main factor in realizing a fair income distribution. In Syria, wageworkers constitute 55.4% of Syrian employees (2,688,171 out of 4,859,949).[3] Therefore, nothing affects as many people as policies on wages and salaries, particularly when a worker's average monthly income is as little as SYP 8,693 (ca. $ 185).[4] The Statistical Abstract of 2007 shows in Table 3/8 that 16% of the employed get salaries of less than SYP 5,000 a month, and 61% get less than SYP 9,000. Those who do get more than SYP 9,000 a month mostly earn it in the public sector (around 52%), whereas their rate in the private sector is no more than 23%. And 9,000 SYP is hardly enough for a decent life.

The Syrian state has expanded employment within the so-called "social employment policy". It set up rigid legislation in favor of workers, which was reflected mainly in tough procedures to dismiss workers. It established labor courts and set minimum level of wages. The legislation required that employers register their employees with the Social Security system, but the application of this legislation is very weak in reality. The Syrian government, however, is moving now towards the liberalization of the labor market and has prepared a new labor draft law that allows for more flexibility in dismissals; this is strongly opposed by the Federation of Trade Unions, but it will ultimately find a way to be enacted.

Objective economic necessities require that the level of wages and salaries is equal to the level that ensures the worker the minimum level of standard of living enabling him to renew his working energy and to support his family in order to produce a new generation of labor force to replace the old one. Nevertheless, this level is neither defined nor fixed; it varies according to time and place and depends on several factors. One is the balance of power between the employers and that of the workers since, if we suppose that total income is fixed, raising th share of profits would be at the expense of wages and vice versa. The elements in this balance include:

1. the workers' level of awareness and organization in syndicates capable of negotiating with employers organizations; it is noticeable that syndicates in Syria are virtually non-existent in the private sector.

2. High rates of unemployment put workers in a weak negotiating position; in Syria today, as a result, some salaries and wages are no more than SYP 3,000 for some private sector workers.

3. Also a factor is state legislation regulating the labor market by setting a minimum level of wages and salaries, and the capability of state institutions to enforce these regulations; it is noticeable that the government in Syria has not effectively forced the private sector to abide by labor legislation, such as minimum wage levels and joining the social security scheme. Only 18.9% of private sector workers are registered in the Social Security program, but mostly not based on their full salaries; since all public sector workers are registered according to the law, i.e. based on their full basic salaries, this gives the private sector an unfair advantage (see table 2.1).

4. The workers' capability to express their demands through strikes is still restricted in Syria. The state still keeps the old restrictions used when it was the major employer; but now that the private sector is the major employer workers should be granted the rights of collective bargaining appropriate to the move toward a market economy.

Besides the balance of power between capital and labour, the second important condition in determining salary and wage levels is the level of development of the national economy. When the added value/income increases, the absolute value of wages will increase even though its proportion compared to profits may not increase. That is to say, when primary economic sectors, such as agriculture and light manufacturing industries that have limited value added, dominate production and when productivity is low whether due to the low level of the technology or because of weak organization, which is the case of Syria today, it will not be possible to substantially raise wages without setting off inflation. However, higher productivity does not mean higher wages unless it is associated with a balanced negotiation capability by labor, otherwise the increase would be transferred to the share of capital i.e. the profits. Therefore, a successful policy to develop the levels of wages and salaries requires the development of economic sectors with higher added values, which require a highly qualified and trained labor force. However, government plans are geared towards increasing the total investment without discriminating in favor of value added industries.[5]

Table 2.1: Number of people insured with the Social Security Establishment[6]

Sector	Number of paid workers (end 2006)	Number of insured workers (August 2007)	Insured people (%)
Public	1,355,763	1,167,963	86.1
Private	1,325,557	251,101	18.9
Total	2,681,320	1,419,064	52.9

Since more than one quarter of the Syrian labor force have government jobs, state policy also plays a major role in formulating the structure and defining the levels of wages and salaries. In general, the average salaries of government officials and employees in government institutions are still higher than those of the private sector, not at the top income levels but because of very low bottom range of wages in the latter. Government policy has also aimed at reducing wage differentials in public employment which has fallen from that of a top level being nine times as much as that of the lowest level at the end of the 1960s to around four times currently. This system pushes highly qualified and competent people to leave public service for the private sector where top positions are much better paid, thus leaving the less competent in the public sector at the expense of government institutions' capacity. How can we understand, for example, that the salary of the general director of the Syrian Petroleum Co., which generates around 45% of the local budgetary resources and around 70% of the foreign exchange budget revenues, does not exceed SYP 18,000; in the same sector Syrian petroleum engineers work for years to gain experience, then the best of them go abroad which involves a big loss to the state.

A big obstacle to addressing low government salaries is the high level of tax evasion in the private sector. The government has periodically increased public sector wages, but this tends to lead to inflation and the decline of purchasing power, a problem which it has not yet solved. It is necessary to reform radically the government salaries and compensation system to increase the maximum levels at the top ranks (to ten times that of the lowest level) in order to retain quality manpower.

Some in the government sector and many in the private one think that raising wages would increase the cost of Syrian products and diminish their competitiveness in foreign markets. They claim controlling wage increases is a way to create job opportunities, and that low wage jobs are better than unemployment. That might be so in some sectors, in the short run, and within a development vision that combines traditional sectors of low wages and while promoting sectors with higher added value as a long run policy. Workers should get fair wages, linked both to the increasing costs of living, but also according to the levels of productivity, since high wages cannot be sustained without high productivity. In order to prevent a conflict between wages and competitiveness, employers should develop applied technology, improve the work organization and/or train the workers. They should link the wage raise to productivity while the worker, on the other side, should show commitment to his duties. This strategy requires investment in research and development, which even at low levels could lead to the production of Syrian products at European specifications and at Chinese prices.

Another factor affecting wages is monetary policy. Policy makers seek to make exports more competitive by reducing the exchange rate of national currency, but because this raises the cost of imports and reduces the purchasing power of wages and salaries, syndicates are usually against this policy or demand wages and salaries increases in exchange. It does not help that Syria imports products at internationally rising prices while its exports earn low prices on international markets, which again can only be addressed by developing higher value-added exports. For many years, Syria had multiple centrally fixed exchange rates; in this way it set a low exchange rate for basic commodities in order to keep their prices low so as to prevent the deterioration of living standards of low-income people, with the government providing the hard currency required for private sector imports. This multiple exchange rate policy is coming to an end, although the government has applied it to defend the Syrian pound exchange rate vs. the USD when it declined to around SYP 52/1 USD in 2003 due largely to international price increases, pushing it up to 48/1 in 2008, which partially helped control the price increases of the last years.

Based on the above analysis, and in order to make wage levels play their positive role in development, growth and equity we recommend the following:

First, the government should enhance the capacity of its institutions to organize the labor market and enforce labor and social security legislation in the private sector including minimum levels of wages and salaries; government intervention is needed to organize the employer/worker relation since workers are the weak party, ensure protection from arbitrary dismissal without giving an absolute guarantee against it and ensure fair compensation, as well as organizing working hours, vacations and annual leaves. At the same time, it is necessary to develop more flexible labor legislation since overly rigid ones encourage slackness in implementation.

Second, there should be a link between levels of wages and prices in order to force the business community to raise productivity by developing technology, improving the management and upgrading research and development. Government planning should prioritize investment in higher value-added industries; it also should continue to defend the Syrian pound exchange rate in order to stabilize consumer prices.

Third, the government should secure pre-vocational and vocational training programs and follow-up qualification programs to change the career or the workplace and career guidance. All that should be done without creating any interference that paralyzes the labor market and deters investors.

The trade unions should develop a program to enhance their presence and role in the private sector in order to defend workers rights; workers should enjoy the right to strike since the private sector is becoming the major employer; the government should oversee collective labor contracts between a company's workers and its management. The government should encouraging the idea of having an elected workers' representative on the boards of big companies to both represent the workers and to help the employer increase productivity and reduce costs through involvement of workers' leagues in discussing the general policy of private companies, and move towards applying the distribution of part of the companies' profits to the workers.

The principle of expanding and diversifying ownership of property

The second main instrument of equity in a social market economy is the diversification of property ownership. The essential issue is that the expansion of production is accompanied by increasing the number of owners, with most Syrians becoming owners of small properties, or shareholders or participants in cooperatives, resulting in a more equitable income distribution. "Property is a Social Responsibility" is a suitable motto in this context because individual interests are viewed within the context of the wider public interest, but not on the liberal assumption that the pursuit of individual interest automatically realizes the public interest. Indeed avoiding monopolies of the means of production requires formulating an overall government policy aiming to encourage a mixed economy having different types of property--big and small private property, co-operative property and state property--with none discriminated against and each allowed to compete with the other. This will make obsolete both policies of expropriation of private property and of privatization of state-owned enterprises, with both extreme positions equally harmful. The concept of business enterprise should not be restricted to the private individual capitalist one, but should include any economic activity regardless of ownership, including the state sector, which should be subject to the same regulations, laws and rules. Additionally, private property should not mean individual property only; it should include private corporate property such as stock property and cooperative property.

The important issue here is not to sacrifice the expansion of the property basis and the realization of social equity to market freedom which creates social polarization. Thus, the state needs to develop a set of programs to protect cooperative forms of private property as discussed below.

Development of cooperative stock companies

We need to encourage "*cooperative stock companies*" in which no shareholder will have the right to hold more than a certain percentage of the shares because holding a high ratio of shares would enable the holder to control the company and its management. All people working for such companies will be shareholders and will get part of their rewards as shares in the company. The current legislation should be developed to include this kind of company and to give them preferential treatment. An example of a non-monopolistic cooperative stock company that might be encouraged would be a third mobile telephone company. The Ministry of Telecommunications and Technology should take the initiative in establishing a stock company in which the Telecommunications Establishment holds 30% of the shares and tens of thousands of citizens hold the remaining 70%. The number of shares held by each shareholder should be limited to avoid monopoly; also, it is possible to develop a system to allocate some shares to the subscribers, or include the value of some shares in the subscription. Some will resist this idea under different pretexts, such as that the company's management will fail and it may be corrupted. Such a company may face serious challenges, but the idea is sound. It would be a publically-owed stock company and not a state-owned one; it elects its management according to the rules practiced in stock companies and they are subject to monitoring and evaluation. This form is widely spread throughout the world and works efficiently and successfully in the free market economies. As is the case in big private sector companies, the company may be managed by experts, or may make a contract with an international company specialized in the management of phone companies. All these choices and others are available and can be a success and generate profits, which would be distributed to tens of thousands of shareholders. Moreover, Syrians are quite capable of operating such companies. MTN, for example, which is the second largest mobile phone operator after Syriatel, (owned by the Trade Unions of South Africa) has 1,500 employees and only seven of them are non-Syrians. Experience proves that the Syrian labor force is able to quickly gain expertise when it works within a suitable environment. If some call for privatization, this is privatization. It breaks the state monopoly and opens the door for the private sector, but it is not the type of privatization desired and sought by some people, where one or a handful of businesspersons monopolize a company generating billion of Syrian pounds annually; rather we seek a company owned by tens of thousands of people. Indeed, this proposal is not to the Minister of Telecommunications and Technology, or to the government, rather it is to the citizens who have a real interest in such projects and should take the initiative and not watch indifferently while others determine their future. The software industry is another field that has a big potential for a cooperative stock company to operate and find markets in the Gulf and Europe. Many examples can be given of companies which, due to many members having a stake in them, enlarge the basis of income distribution and create new job opportunities.

Cooperative property development

The cooperative sector grew up the 19th and 20th centuries, with thinkers such as Robert Owen preaching cooperative socialism. Cooperation played a prominent role in many countries, especially in agriculture, but in the socialist movement, especially the Soviet one, it adopted the "state property" approach. However, after the failure and collapse of the Soviet experience, cooperative property is being reconsidered in modern societies.

Cooperation has not played a significant role in Syria, except in the housing and agricultural sectors. The state fostered state owned property and people did not take initiatives to establish their own cooperative sector. Even the parties that adopted socialism and social justice have not paid real attention to the importance of developing this sector. However, the under-utilized potential of cooperation nominates it to play a significant socioeconomic role in the future. Indeed, there are many forms of establishing cooperative activities, but popular activism is the major source of cooperation.

Many circumstances have hindered this sector and that is why it has such a limited role in Syria. The unsuccessful experiences of cooperation in Syria will make it difficult convincing people of its potential. Thus, the first condition of success is to assess the previous experience. The major lesson learnt is that cooperatives have not been voluntary ones, rather they have been imposed by the government through a kind of bureaucratic control so the farmers rejected them, and they remained empty forms. The second condition is to develop a new law of cooperatives benefiting from similar laws in Western countries instead of the current one that is taken from the former socialist countries. Such a new law should include some incentives to encourage establishing cooperatives. It should also establish a new institution to foster cooperation, based on the principles of the private sector and subject to the law, i.e. cooperatives should work according to the principles of market economy, supply/demand, quality and price competition, etc. The government could support such an institution financially without intervening in its management. Also important would be the training of a group of competent people who believe in cooperation to run this sector in Syria, provided that they receive wages similar to their equivalents in the private sector. A support program funded by donors and by the government would finance the establishment of the cooperative sector, train its staff and carry out a media promotional campaign. The role of an impartial judiciary would be to guard it against the misuse of the trust granted to cooperative staff. The most important condition is to foster some models that set an example and develop experience. The following are fields in which cooperatives would be particularly beneficial.

Consumer cooperatives could be an effective response to the wave of price increases throughout the world, including Syria, and the high rates of profit achieved by intermediate activities. The people of a town, or of a quarter in a city, could establish a consumer cooperative. Such cooperatives can connect producers directly to consumers who will get the goods at lower prices provided they are sold at reasonable margins of profit. Such cooperatives could rent from the Ministry of Economy the retail halls of the General Establishment for Consumption instead of renting them to big businesspersons, who are actively trying to appropriate them.

The housing cooperative sector in Syria has accumulated some very good experience. It has provided houses to hundreds of thousands of families. Notable is the experience of the Dummar Housing Cooperative Project, where several housing cooperatives gathered in the mid 1970s and developed a housing project of 5000 apartments, which became one of the main housing areas in Damascus. It was a success in spite of the difficulties it encountered, especially as the initial idea was that the project itself undertakes the building works. The experience of this project is worthy of study and replication but, unfortunately, it has been repeated neither in Damascus nor in other cities.

The state has supported the housing cooperative sector through allocating residential lands to the cooperatives at low prices and through establishing a specialized bank for real estate lending at easy conditions for cooperatives, whose activity, along with individual building of houses, dominated most of the housing industry. The role of housing cooperation in

Syria is threatened by the rise of private real estate companies, Arab and Syrian. These companies will use their influence to compete for the best lands for building. Therefore, it is important for people to maintain this important sector to provide them with housing.

Syria also has experience with agricultural cooperatives. Although this has not gone beyond carrying out some administrative procedures jointly, such as getting loans in kind and cash loans, receiving seeds, and the like, it has great potentials to address many current and future problems. The first problem has been the fragmentation of land to small and very smallholdings that are not efficiently exploitable by individuals working alone. Second, there is the need to expand the use of agricultural mechanization and to change to capital-intensive farming in order to increase land productivity. This can happen only through the expansion of capacity through pooling resources in cooperatives. These cooperatives could promote the introduction of new crops and make contracts with consumer cooperatives or with food industry firms to market their products under good conditions. They also could establish workshops to sort, wrap and package the products, which increases the added value and profitability. Additionally, they could establish small food industries like the associations of grape farmers in Cyprus, who have a plant for manufacturing wine from their grapes.

Developing properties of municipalities and local community organizations

Municipalities can extend their property alone or in cooperation with local partners. They can encourage the establishment of cooperative companies of the residents by commissioning them to deliver services such as cleaning, maintenance, and the like. They may form partnerships with the local people to establish a company to exploit tourist attractions in a town and its surroundings. Additionally, they may form partnerships with trade unions to establish a cooperative company to implement any kind of business or industries. Coalitions between a municipality and civil society associations have great potential to establish service companies and businesses that expand the base of property and income distribution. The first requirement for the success of such a sector is that the municipal council represents and is accountable to the local citizens and that the people elect the mayor who should be a local citizen.

Developing trade unions' property

Among the so far wasted potentials is the lost opportunity to establish companies owned by syndicates, either by trade unions or by professional association. In Syria, there are a relatively large number of syndicates, whose members constitute a large proportion of the population (see table 2.2).

Table 2.2: Syndicate membership

Syndicate	Members
204 trade unions with 188 social aid funds	808,419
Bar Association	19,346
Association of Engineers	94,606
Association of Agronomists	24,220
Association of Teachers	294,831
Association of Physicians	27,636
Association of Dentists	13,766
Association of Pharmacists	12,192
Association of Artists	n.a.
Association of Journalists	n.a.
Authors Union	n.a.
Total = 808,419 (trade unions) and 486,597 (other associations)	1,295,019

Source: Central Bureau of Statistics, The Syrian Statistical Abstract, 2007.

These unions could establish specialized companies related to their field of activity. The trade unions have made several investments, but their returns were negligible because their management suffered from the same bureaucratic nature as the government administration. Investments of the Association of Engineers have been better in comparison, but remained limited. Professional associations, especially the Association of Engineers, but also those of physicians, pharmacists, lawyers and teachers have accumulated large unutilized funds which they deposit at banks where they get limited returnsl these could be used to start companies.

Cooperative stock companies for distribution set up by trade unions
Trade unions in partnership with professional associations could also establish a cooperative non-monopolistic stock company to distribute consumer goods, e.g. by establishing chains of retail stores throughout Syria. They could contribute to a part of the capital and allow the other part to be subscribed by the members and even by the public. Such a company would have the elements of potential success, basically, the number of members and around 1.5 million potential customers, which is an important market that no private company has. Such a company may, and perhaps must, make a contract with a specialized management company or with a series of warehouses worldwide to develop a complete operation and management system to ensure efficient performance, which attracts members and non-members as customers. A cooperative stock company could also be formed to establish hospitals, in which the Associations of Physicians and Pharmacists, and perhaps others participate. They could also establish a cooperative stock company for medicine manufacturing, drug distribution warehouses and pharmacies. This industry is flourishing in Syria; now, it covers about 90% of Syria's need for medicines and also exports to dozens of countries. A cooperative stock company for engineering studies could be initiated by the Association of Engineers, or jointly with other associations. Syria lacks such a company, while a large number of small offices with limited capabilities practice this profession. Syrians are masters in this kind of services, and the World Wide Web provides an important opportunity to provide these services from Syria directly to the world, notably to markets in the Gulf States and Europe, where labor costs are high.

Developing state property
Despite the attack waged by liberalism on state property and the efforts made to attribute all evils to it, the argument that the state should not own at all is a typical ideological one refuted by reality. On the other hand, we do not consider state property a social one owned by people collectively since it is the government, and perhaps only the minister and some ministerial staff, that takes decisions about state property.

This leads us to the issue of the state's investment policy. The government's allocations for investment in the state sector are declining with negative effects on the development process and the government's capability to carry out its duties, especially since the major part of public investment expenditure is on government buildings, hospitals, schools, universities and their equipment, not on factories and companies. The treasury faces a clear problem that needs to be addressed urgently. It owns about 250 companies and economic establishments, whose contribution to the treasury falls yearly. Eight companies, mostly oil firms, provide around 100 billion SYP/year, while 242 companies and government establishment provide only 38 billion SYP/year because most of them are loss-making and a large part of the surplus of profit making companies is taken to cover the deficits of other companies. Additionally, in 2008, the state budget revenues were estimated to amount to about SYP 400 billion in 2008 and the expenditures SYP 600 billion. This is in spite of reducing investment expenditure, which traditionally was half the budget, to 38% of the total expenditure.[7]

The second issue is the government's inability to reform the public sector, which is being left to deteriorate further. It is not a matter of lacking solutions, as there are many and the matter has been discussed repeatedly in detail but a government decision is needed. The author has participated in more than one government committee to reform the public sector and developed more than one detailed diagnosis and prescription for designing a new management for it that guarantees its financial and administrative independence and to raise its competitiveness in an open market. Among the main recommendations are: to conduct a comprehensive diagnosis of each public sector company's financial and asset status; to distinguish on this basis companies that the state wants to keep for strategic reasons, such as cereals, fuel, water and electricity and to reform these and to dissolve companies that are non-viable and unable to compete in the market. Reforming public companies involves restructuring them through mergers and giving them management independence to allow them flexibility similar to private firms. Furthermore, they should be exempted from the laws and legislation of the administrative sector, including the system of contracts, salaries, compensation and others. For one time only, the treasury should cancel their debts and provide start up capital. An agency to manage the government's investments in the public sector companies should be created to work according to the standards of holding companies in the private sector. The capital accounts of public companies should be opened for investment by other public companies, private sector partners and citizens, with the situation of each company considered separately. The companies' subordination to the Central Authority for Control and Inspection should be ended, keep them under the supervision of the Financial Control Body only. The companies should develop their internal systems to operate according to market rules. A program should be set up to address the problem of surplus staff in the governmental economic sector; this could be dealt with by employing part of them in other reformed companies or through paying compensation to those wishing to leave work or take early retirement. In all cases, costs would be much less than in the current system. Reforming the public sector will save huge amounts of money for the state and change the public sector from an institution that wastes public money to one that supports production, feeds the treasury and creates jobs.

Developing small and medium properties

This sector plays today a big role in the economies of developed countries. It is, also, anticipated to play such a role in Syria, where for many years it was the dominant sector since the policy of nationalizing large companies discouraged their growth. All agricultural properties became small and medium ones after the land reform. The state also fostered the small sector through state banks: thus, the Popular Credit Bank was created in 1966 to grant easy loans to small traders, artisans, professionals and low-income people at an interest rate ranging between 7% and 9%; likewise, the Agricultural Bank makes loans to farmers at low interest rates ranging between 4.5% and 6%. In the transport sector most passenger and cargo vehicles are individually owned; transport companies appeared only after enacting Law 10 of 1991. Private construction contracting companies did business mostly with the state and, at the same time, were at a disadvantage in competing with the state construction sector. Also, the small sector controlled real estate activity entirely, while large real estate companies appeared in Syria only as late as 2006. The absence of big chain companies meant that the small and micro sector controlled the retail trade and only in the last two years big malls started to appear, and their market share is still small though anticipated to grow.

According to the "General Census of Population and Housing, Enterprise Stocktaking and Agricultural Census", carried out by the Central Bureau of Statistics in 2004, the number of enterprises operating in Syria was estimated to be around 600,000, with micro enterprises of less than five workers constituting around 500,000 of these. The private sector owns 92% of the economic enterprises operating in Syria. 95.5% of private properties are individual ones, while only 4.5% are corporate properties. Thus, family, micro and small enterprises form 99.5% of total private enterprises, with 96% for micro enterprises and 3.5% for small enterprises (see table 2.3).

Table 2.3: Distribution of micro and small enterprises by economic activity

Economic Activity	Less than 5 workers		5-14 workers	
	Number	%	Number	%
Agriculture & Fishing	9,089	1.80	434	2.34
Manufacturing	81,475	16.13	10,309	55.47
Trade	316,521	62.68	4,491	24.16
Restaurants	12,855	2.55	1,038	5.58
Transport and storing	7,338	1.45	540	2.91
Real estates	20,531	4.07	300	1.61
Education	1,052	0.21	504	2.71
Health	19,691	3.90	220	1.18
Social services	31,283	6.19	403	2.17
Other sectors	5,179	1.03	347	1.87
Total	505,014	100	18,586	100

Current reform policies threaten the role of small enterprises as establishing large companies would drive small businesspeople from the market. The solution is not to return to the policy of discouraging big investments, but to encourage small investors to merge into cooperatives or cooperative companies, which combines economies of scale with broad-based ownership. The other side is the development of a package of policies to support small and medium enterprises, which Syria began several years ago. Accordingly, we think that the state must conduct a comprehensive study on small and micro enterprises and develop a clear strategy for the specific roles that these enterprises can play within specific areas, identify clearly the promising sectors for investment, and develop a package of commercial and tax policies that encourage small enterprises' investment. Another issue that needs addressing is the extreme geographical concentration of businesses, with about half of them (49%) located in the three big governorates: Damascus, Rural Damascus and Aleppo, reflecting, to some extent, the geographical distribution of income. Therefore, it is very important that the government launches an effective program to develop the other regions, especially the Eastern Region (see table 2.4).

Table 2.4: Geographical distribution of micro and small enterprises

Governorate	Less than 5 workers		5-14 workers	
	Number	%	Number	%
Damascus & Rural Damascus	138,147	27.36	5,465	29.40
Aleppo	109,694	21.72	7,723	41.55
Homs	50,162	9.93	1,094	5.89
Hama	30,596	6.06	873	4.70
Other Governorates	176,415	34.93	3,431	18.46
Total	505,014	100	18,586	100

Enhancing medium and large private investment

The national private medium and large investment will play an increasing role under reform, with the legislative, regulatory and institutional structure, including consultation mechanisms with the private sector aimed to tap the great potential for such investment. A comprehensive development strategy with clear priorities is essential to direct the private sector's investments in a way that promotes job creation, develops the structure of the economy, raises productivity, introduces industries of higher added value and develops exports. This requires that local medium and large private sector enterprises restructure and rid themselves of the distortions created in the past in order to be competitive at the regional and global levels.

This sector can take two distinguishable forms. Large individual private firms, whether owned by an individual or a family or a stock company owned by a small number of shareholders, is the major, if not the dominant, form in Syria today. It will continue to exist in all areas of investment open for it within the social market economy. The expansion of this form of property and its future dominance, particularly through the decline of small firms, threatens to lead to a polarization of wealth. Current reforms are encouraging this sector, and while this is required, little attention is given to other sectors as a result of large companies' strength and ability to influence and exploit globalization. Since leaving it to the free market would, no doubt, lead to monopoly and polarization, there is a need to strengthen other forms to achieve a social balance and higher level of social equity.

A type of large firm that should be encouraged is the *traditional stock company* which gives small savers the opportunity to invest their saving through a stock market. This type of companies started to grow early in Syria, beginning with the establishment of Dummar Cement Factory in the early 1930s. In the 1950s many such companies were founded. However, after the nationalization measures new companies started to take the form of family or limited liability companies with a small number of partners. Only with the new reforms are stock companies starting to re-emerge offering their shares for public underwriting, beginning with the establishment of private banks and insurance companies. Law 61 of 2007 was issued to facilitate the transformation of family companies into closed stock companies which prepared the way for their conversion into stock companies offering part of their shares for public underwriting. Income Tax Law 24 of 2003, amended by Law 51 of 2006, was issued to reduce corporate income taxes to between 14% and 28%, which is low by international standards. 14% applies to stock companies, which offer more than half of their shares for public underwriting, and 28% to all other types of companies. Also, the long-awaited stock exchange will play a role in promoting this type of company. The stock market can contribute to providing companies with funds, while it also expands the basis of property and increases the number of owners, thereby broadening the basis of income distribution.

However, stock companies which do not set strict ceilings on the shares any individual can own will fall under the control of one or a few investors. For example, the experiences of stock companies, which have an ownership ceiling of 5% of shares per investor, show that an investor may evade the rules by buying more than 5% through his children or brothers so that he, under a few names, controls the company. In addition to that, he manages the shares of other companies and exploits the company for the interests of a few. A related problem which allows such practices is the complete absence of any supervisory agencies or auditing institutions, or even an effective honest judiciary to protect small shareholders. Syrians' refusal to buy the shares of some companies, which have announced their conversion into stock companies, expressed their lack of confidence in them. By contrast, the experience of private banks and insurance companies, which have non-Syrian strategic partners, apply auditing and transparency standards, and care about their reputation, show that the Syrians are keen to buy shares. This deficiency requires urgent treatment so small investors will have confidence in stock companies.

The principle of the private sector's social contribution

In the modern market economy, companies' social care programs play an increasing role in redistributing part of the income. Today companies around the world boast about their social programs, such as scholarships to excellent students, sponsoring cultural activities, donations to social associations of people with special needs, environment protection programs, historical sites conservation programs, empowerment of the poor programs and so on. This transformation, which is characterized by the declining role of the government's social protection, has obvious ideological meanings but is nevertheless a positive contribution. But only a few Syrian private companies have such programs today and their contributions are often restricted to charities that provide food, clothes and medicine to the poor, which is a traditional form of charity.

The predominant contradiction today is between a company, which is privately owned and managed, and its character as a social institution in whose production hundreds, thousands or even tens of thousands are involved, and to whose success and failure many interests are linked, including those of its workers, the consumers of its products or services, and its suppliers of raw materials and services. They are affected as well by its commitment to its duties and financial, productive and social obligations and the like. Mitigating this contradiction takes place within a social market economy through wider participation of the workers and stakeholders in the company's decisions, without affecting the property ownership. Thus, increasing the social nature of private companies is an issue that is wider than mere social care programs despite their importance.

There are two approaches that can be taken in this regard. Companies can be given tax incentives to develop various social programs. Recently, the income tax law included giving companies the possibility to make donations to public organizations and non-profitable private ones of no more than 3% of the company's profits. Some companies set an example by establishing social programs, such as allocating scholarships for students, arranging training courses for the unemployed, establishing a clinic in a quarter or a district, contributing to cleaning the environment in a certain area, or supporting a specific cultural program, etc. These are voluntary programs benefiting the company's reputation. Beyond this, big companies can be encouraged to become social institutions in addition to being profit-making ones for their owners. The workers could be given a stake in the company through shares and by representation in the company's annual general assembly. The company should also be subject to a public social review in order to assess its not just its annual economic performance but also its meeting of its social obligations. This review includes the way it deals with its workers, their rights, salaries and incentives and registration in the Social Security system, their fulfillment of tax obligations, as well as product quality. This, also, includes transparent disclosure that it has not practiced any activities in contradiction with the laws and has neither evaded any taxes or fees, nor smuggled goods or paid bribes. This would be a community review rather than a governmental one and it should be for the good of the company as it provides the company with an ethically valuable testimony. This should be a factor when the company bids for government contracts and in its dealings with banks, as it is a "clean company". The private sector's initiative to launch such programs would be an indicator of its ability to be up to national needs.

The principal of an active society

A social market economy cannot succeed without an active civil society. The economy is an arena for both the conflict and cooperation of interests; the parties in market relations can be clustered in the following major actors: Employers are represented by organizations, such as chambers of commerce, industry and tourism. They are a minority in terms of numbers, but have the greater power due to their financial strengths and great effect on the market; the workers, of both the state and private sectors, constitute the biggest mass in terms of number, which gives them the potential to have influence which, to be realized requires they organize themselves in parties, syndicates, and community organizations for farmers, students, women, etc. A big critical mass in between consists of small property holders. The state is an arbiter and organizer of the society and is subject to pressures from the actors.

The success of social market economy requires an active community that makes the workers and small property holders able to express their interests. It also requires a clear governmental vision and ability to manage negotiations among the actors so as to maintain balance with a view to realize its socioeconomic goals. To organize a dialogue between the parties a socioeconomic council should be formed containing the representatives of the three main parties. This council should be a platform to discuss and agree on the rules that maintain balance and stimulate holistic socioeconomic development.

We need an active society to overcome the barriers that would obstruct the social market model, particularly that of corruption and misuse of power. The main reason that prevents people from participation in cooperatives, private collective properties and properties of municipalities, trades unions and the state is their fear that corruption and misuse of power by those who assume the management of these organizations may eat up the participants' money and efforts. The government's agencies and the judiciary, in their current status, are unable to protect the rights of stakeholders because corruption can easily achieve its purposes. Therefore, people believe that those who misuse the powers delegated to them by members of companies and associations, shareholders, etc. are unaccountable, which will block people from joining cooperatives or investing in private collective property. This diminishes the emergence of these types of property and weakens the cornerstone of property expansion. Moreover, there is the Syrian citizens' individualism and reluctance to participate, which is the result of culture, on one hand, and of lack of trust from the damaging practices they suffered for decades.

The establishing of a social market economy and the realization of development requires an active anti-corruption program led by an anti-corruption agency; a reform of the judiciary to combat internal corruption and enhance its efficiency; the separation of the legislative, executive and judicial powers -especially removing the executive power's control over the other two powers-, and a wide participation by the people, particularly with regard to the establishment of cooperatives and cooperative companies. Here the role of trade unions, professional associations, civil organizations and political parties, which were and still are inactive in this regard, is crucial. The media also plays a crucial role in promotion and mobilization. Society should have a proactive role rather than being satisfied with letting government take the initiatives: a social market economy should have initiatives from the three parties: government, business community and civil society.

Conclusion

History is proof that neither a monopolizing state and weak society, nor an economy monopolied by giant corporations and a weak state are the answer to development. Humanity is asking how to couple economic growth and social justice.

If Syria is not to make the transition to a neo-liberal version of a market economy by default and hence to suffer growing social inequality, a "smart" state must take an active role. It must deploy its macro-economic policies in a way that is sensitive to the social distributional consequences, must organize and regulate the labour market and must promote a wide distribution of property ownership. So far, its reforms have largely neglected this social side. If a social market economy is to emerge a corrective in this policy tangent is in order.

But how could the ideas in this proposal be realized in practice? It needs a suitable legal framework, an efficient and uncorrupted judiciary and bureaucracy and a change in conservative mentalities. But this, too, is a matter of a struggle of classes and interests. As such, a suitable outcome is only possible with an active civil society including freedom of expression, the right to organize and to strike and a party law. President Asad promised the issuance of a party law and the Syrians are waiting for that.

---

[1] Dr. Issam Azzaem, interviewed by Castro Nassi, *Qassyoun*, 21/07/2005, retrieved from *All-4-Syria*.

[2] Although the government speaks a lot about participation and the social aspects of reform in order to deflect accusations that it prioritizes the business community and profit, analyzing the policies applied and the results achieved give clear evidence that the social side is ignored; moreover, this is not a coincidence but a deliberate policy that is not likely to change.

[3] Refer to the *Statistical Abstract of 2007*, table 3/5.

[4] Refer to the *Syrian Economic Trends Bulletin*, Volume 1, Issue1, Oct. 2007 (ISMF- SPC).

[5] For more useful details refer to UNDP (2004), "Report on Education and Human Development in Syria", particularly pages 136-143.

[6] The Social Security Establishment Report of 2006, and *Economy and Transport Magazine*, February, 2008.

[7] The actual investment expenditure has not exceeded 60% of the allocations.

Appendix: Debates on the Political Economy of Reform

Proceedings of the Conference, "Syria in a Changing World" Damascus 7-9 November 2008

Sponsored jointly by the Centre for Syrian Studies University (CSS), St. Andrews, and the Orient Centre for International Studies (OCIS), Damascus

The following reports on the papers given at the 2008 conference in Damascus and the discussion that accompanied them. The papers fall into four categories:

1) The historical context which provides some insights into the background to the current situation in Syria, including the on-going negative role of the US and the heritage of Hafiz al-Asad.

2) Debates over the role of the state in reform, the politics of reform, the nature of the social market economy which is the official goal of transition, the obstacles to its achievement and its social consequences.

3) Reform developments in two key sectors of the economy, agriculture and industry.

4) The external context of reform, including relations with Lebanon, Turkey and Europe and the development of the peace process.

1) The historical context

Syria under the Liberal Regime and the impact of US policy (Sami Moubayed, Kalamoun University)

The first problem of independent Syria was to assert government control over its territory and ward off subversion from neighbours. But the first elite was urban centred and feared strengthening the army to accomplish this would threaten the regime, especially as there was plotting in the army by Jordan and Iraq. There was a proposal to dissolve and reconstruct the army by recruitment from Damascene elite families and the Minister of Defence was told to weaken the army. As a result of this and corruption in army supplying, Syria was unprepared for the war of 1948. The defeat cost the elite its legitimacy.

Then the regime faced pressures from the US and Israel. There were disputes with the US over Syria's closing of the Tapline oil pipe from Saudi Arabia over the Palestine issue, over the role of the communists in Syria and over the conditions of truce with Israel. One of the first CIA operations led to the coup by Husni al-Zaim against Quwatli after which a truce was signed, Tapline reopened and the communists repressed.

In the 1954-58 period, a golden age of pluralism, the US again attempted regime change through coups. When the Ba'th and communists won seats in the elections Washington was alarmed; Syria was also accused of meddling in Lebanon. US interference strengthened the nationalist-leftist forces and pushed Syria toward the USSR. The parallels between this and contemporary US-Syria relations are striking.

Comment of Ibrahim Yakhour: Quwatli assumed the role of za'im, more than just the presidency and hence the opportunity to have a modern constitutional state was lost. He wanted to be the leader of the Damascene bourgeoisie that looked down on those from outside Damascus, especially the peasants.

Syria under Hafiz al-Asad (George Jabbur, former advisor of the late president)

Hafiz was the most important figure in modern Syria. His personal attributes were important to his leadership. He was upright and modest in his personal behaviour, a hard worker who worked very long hours, and a good listener who did not interrupt others. He talked to subordinates individually over the telephone rather than face-to-face together. In domestic politics his ideal was to forge a consensus, co-opting non-Ba'this into his government.

Comment of Nizar Mayhoob: Hafiz established Syria's regional and international stature. The legacy of Hafiz has been used under Bashar to survive the external turbulence and pressures. Such pressures exerted on another regime would have led to capitulation.

2) State and Reform

Syria, Post-populist State (Samir al-Taqi, Director of OCIS)

In the populist era there was an alliance of social forces with the state, initially the peasants, but later the private sector was included in a regulated way. The state was over-powerful and too autonomous of the alliance of social forces in its coalition. Now, under pressure of economic problems and globalization, the social contract is being changed to facilitate economic growth. The neo-liberal shock therapy model has elsewhere had high costs or has ended in disaster and Syria's production relations and forces are not yet able to be competitive on the global market. So Syria is pursuing a gradual transition, being selective in adopting from other experiences, in order to find its own model. The current situation is that there is some separation of the political structure from economic affairs and property is more secure. The insurance and banking sectors are developing well and the black market declining.

Comment of Samir Seifan: the hierarchical state both protects and burdens the economy, which is a contradiction. What explains Syria's slow, selective reform? The state finds it hard to renege on the social contract and to favour the rich. Also the state lacks experience with market regulation. External pressures preoccupied the leadership; but with their relaxation, its focus is again on domestic affairs. The bureaucracy is unwieldy and opposes reform, which threatens its interests. Subsidies and social spending, though a burden, cannot be withdrawn without social shocks and has to be accompanied by a salaries policy. This is hard to manage with oil revenues going down. The crony capitalist private sector also is not very competitive.

Comment: In the Arab countries the period of revolutionary legitimacy went on too long at the expense of developing institutional legitimacy.

Comment: Should economic or political reform come first? If political change goes too fast, you get collapse, as in the Soviet case; if political reform lags you get the predatory state, as in Zaire. A middle way would be increased rule of law and participation constrained by the needs of stability.

Comment: we need reform of the judiciary if we are to get investment. It now takes 5-10 years to get a judgment. You have to give people security of ownership. International arbitration is very costly. We need coherent laws, too, and institutions to prepare laws like the Library of Congress in the US. We need codification of the laws and less contradiction among them. Fewer and better laws is the better approach. We need good media in order for the public to be aware of the laws.

A Syrian Model of a Social Market Economy (Samir Seifan, Director of Arab Development Consultants, Damascus)

Syria's reform is being implemented without a strategy, facing resistance from vested interests and suffering from administrative weaknesses. As a result the poor are being victimized. What is needed is a merit bureaucracy to drive reform.

A proper model of a social market economy needs an effective market to succeed, with government using fiscal and monetary policy rather than direct intervention. Indicative planning should encourage movement from low value to more high value production using more technology. There has to be a mixed economy, with a public sector concentrated in fields that don't compete with the private sector and encouragement of a cooperative sector. The private sector firms should have to contribute to health and education and social insurance for their workers; the trade unions have to be activated as stakeholders in firms.

Comment of Nabil Marzouk: The social market economy in Syria is just a slogan and has no practical content. A social market economy has to be differentiated from a neo-liberal economy, which is what officials are currently pursuing through de-regulation. For a social market economy to work there has to be some balance of power but the unions and the state are too weak. Cooperatives can't work in a market economy, which inevitably leads to concentration of ownership. Only profit seeking, not social responsibility drives firms in a market economy.

Comment: In Syria we have the worst of socialist and liberal economies. What is happening is just the empowerment of capital at the expense of labor, but the unions and parties are silent. No official can say no to investors was raised as a slogan of the regime. To have a balance we need reform of the judiciary and a free press. Also we need competition on the market, which is lacking. The current policy is encouraging industrialists to become traders.

Comment: The government team does not believe in the social part of the market economy. The prerequisites of the social market system are lacking. What about restoring the law on 25% of profits going to workers?

Social Consequences of Reform (Yasin Haj Salah, al-Hiyat; separately solicited paper)

A new bourgeoisie, made up of sons of officials, has emerged and under Bashar has achieved independence from the state. Despite the official slogan of a social market economy, in fact neo-liberalism is being promoted. The wealthy get more freedom and the regime slogan was that any official that said no to an investor would be dismissed while workers and ordinary Syrians face repression. As the social contract is abandoned, the impoverishment of people pushes them into reliance on local communities--sect and tribe. The extreme poverty of the pre-revolutionary period is coming back; one commentator speaks of the "Beirutization" of Damascus. The middle class is squeezed since salaries are not enough to live on. The unions, the National Progressive Front, and some figures on the party Regional Command blame Abdullah Dardari, deputy Prime Minister of Economy, the architect of economic liberalization and have called for an end to this policy and for preserving the social gains of the revolution.

Administrative Reform in Syria (Saam Dalleh)

The civil administration is under pressure to reform. Bashar's presidential acceptance speech stressed this, as did the resolutions of the Ba'th party 10th regional congress and the 10th Five-year plan. We have more demanding and aware citizens from whom you cannot hide much. The new economic environment requires a suitable modernized administration. The new style is that government should only intervene in the economy when necessary to correct problems.

The bureaucracy is oversized and centralized and puts its own needs over those of citizens. It lacks skills and experience; strategic objectives are lost because bureaucratic feudalism frustrates coordination. Personal loyalty is put over merit recruitment; there is a weakness in information and statistics due to lack of IT; corruption is a problem. Reform requires developing human resources, fighting corruption and bringing in new technology such as IT.

Comment by Talal Abboud: The core problem is the lack of effective taxation, hence low salaries that encourages corruption. Big investors are evading taxes and few companies have auditing practices.

Dilemmas of the Politics of Transition (General Discussion)

How is the transition conceptualized? In the 10th party congress there were debates over whether to say the goal was transition to a market economy but others insisted on the social side without being clear what it entailed. Ideally, the transition to the market economy is to be accompanied by social protections. President Bashar al-Asad said that we are free to take what we want and reject what we want from outside models. There is a dispute over whether the public sector should be maintained but not over the need for state regulation. The regime, and especially the security forces, sees the risk of deepening liberalization and is aware of the grumbling among the public.

Why in practice is there neither a real market economy nor social protections? One answer is that state capacity building takes time. Another is that the distribution of burdens and benefits in the transition will depend on the social balance of power and to ensure an equitable transition you have to empower people politically. In any liberalizing country crony capitalists can hijack the benefits and corruption exaggerates the inequalities produced by a market economy. In China, there was also growing corruption and inequality but there was enough growth to buffer the cost.

Populist welfare is being retracted and the government seems unable to protect workers and peasants from the pain of transition. There are not funds available for social protections because oil revenue has declined while taxation of new wealth has lagged. Tax collection is hindered by firms' lack of disclosure of earnings, lack of IT and databases and the corruption of the tax collectors. There has, however, been a real improvement in tax collection.

In the short term, liberalization inflicts pain and until investment produces jobs there are no benefits; all the people experience is price rises and unemployment. The Minister of Labor says the law provides that the private sector should be unionized but only 14% of workers are. There is a draft labor law on more flexibility in firing, needed to assure investors; but the unions have been stalling it for two years, wanting in exchange social safety nets. A few factories provide social services to keep good employees but most businessmen that contribute to charity build mosques rather than hospitals.

The world financial crisis may undermine the reformers. Although Syria is too un-integrated into the world economy to be immediately affected by bank collapses, it will be affected by the consequent deep recession. This could lead to a fall in the prices of imports but will also slow investment inflows and development aid. Syria should learn the lesson from the crisis and regulate bank lending and the inflow and outflow of currencies. In fact, Syrian banks may be *too* prudent in insisting on such high security for lending that lending is too low to stimulate investment.

At this point, there are not many believers in a market economy in either the elites, the press or the population. But liberalization cannot be reversed because entrenched interests in favour of it are too powerful. The current economic team could be made the scapegoat but the course will not be reversed although it could be slowed or stalled.

3) Reform in Key Economic Sectors

The Agricultural Sector (Atieh al-Hindi, Ministry of Agriculture)
Syria has moved from being an importing to exporting country in agriculture. Cultivated area and food calorie intake have also grown. But Syria has suffered from recent drought, with 2008 experiencing only one quarter of usual rainfall. There is a water deficit. In regard to Euphrates water, Turkey releases an average of 500 million cu/meters/second when we want this to be a minimum as sometimes the amount released is insufficient. Agriculture was liberalized; now only tobacco, sugar beet and cotton are marketed by the state [grains used to be state marketed]; central planning has been abandoned for indicative planning.

Problems not yet addressed include the fragmentation of holdings under high population growth, which means investment on holdings is low and most agricultural bank loans are short term ones for financing seasonal inputs.

GAFTA allows imports of agricultural products from other Arab countries but Syria has also been able to export and it has benefited more than the competition hurt it. Our agricultural trade balance was positive till 2005 after which drought has hurt production and it has turned negative.

Comment of Munzar Khaddam: Misuse of water is a chronic problem. Compared to Jordan, our modern irrigation methods have lagged. Fragmentation of ownership is an obstacle to modern irrigation, but the state made it worse by distributing state farms to their employees. Because we don't use all our share of Euphrates water, it is exported to Iraq (Syria takes 42% and Iraq 58% of water released by Turkey). Only 55% of our fertilizer is produced domestically. We have 1000 agricultural extension units but this is hidden unemployment as they do little. Loans of the agricultural bank have decreased 40%. Bad agricultural marketing practices continue, with bad products hidden under good ones. The EU agreement will demand harmonization of standards in agriculture that no Syrian peasant can comply with.

Comment: There needs to be laws to stop urban encroachment on agricultural land.

Syrian Industry (Fuad Lahham, formerly of Ministry of Industry)

Syrian industry is in big trouble and we need it more than ever in a post-oil era. The contribution of industry to GNP has fallen as low as 7% (compared to 20% in Egypt) and is mostly light or semi-manufactured goods with limited value added and technology used.

Syria had a good start in industrialization in the fifties, with 150 share-holding companies and a good location. After nationalization, the private sector exited or downsized. The public sector failed because the priority was social (e.g. employment), while external rent buffered it from the need to be efficient; the quality of investments of this rent was flawed owing to poor feasibility studies, with 60% of new industries inoperative in the 1980s; cadres are poor. Public firms are losing money and only the monopolies are profitable. The public sector implements only 20% of its plan goals. The public sector has not been reformed, with reform still a matter discussed by committees because there is no political will to do so. The government should strengthen the better public firms.

As for the private sector, there are also weaknesses. Firms are mostly family based, relying n relatives, limited in size, evading the law e.g. on taxes, with only a few modern plants up to international standards and few joint stock companies. Indeed, industrialists are becoming traders. Tariff protection has not yet been phased out and the coming implementation of trade agreements could destroy industry since industrial rehabilitation is not accompanying the opening to trade as it did in Tunisia, which was successful in adapting its industry. GAFTA exemptions are given to undeserving firms. Studies on the modernization of industry, which were incorporated into the 10th 5-Year Plan, remain unimplemented. Some 36 textile companies out of 24,000 are being modernized.

Comment: Was there really a consensus on a plan of action of industrial reform which went unimplemented? Or was it a lack of the needed skills and financing to implement it?

4) Syria's International Relations

The Regional Context of Reform (Marwan Kabalan)

Syria needs a foreign policy and external environment compatible with internal reform needs. Regional conflicts obstruct reform while foreign policy has been used to get economic resources to avoid reform. Economic aid makes one dependent, even though Syria never accepted strings on its aid. In the Cold war, Soviet and Arab aid delayed reforms; the end of this has some benefits in that it creates the need to be more productive within and to export more. Bashar has tried to use the EU agreements to leverage reform within until this was put on hold by the deterioration of external relations with the failure of the peace process, the war in Iraq and the crisis in Lebanon. In this crisis, regime survival was at stake and reform was put on hold. With the pressures now relieved, the situation for reform has improved.

Syria-Lebanon Relations (Hamidi al-Abdullah)

Syrian-Lebanese relations are unique, but they have been weakened and Syria's ten years there did not improve them. Many of Syria's allies, such as Hariri and Junblatt, deserted it. At the level of identity there is a lack of consensus among Lebanese on an Arab nationalist identity; rather identity is Lebanese and even the Sunnis don't talk as if they were Arab.

Economic relations are weak, in part because Lebanon is based on free trade and Syria on protection for industry, the origin of the original break in the Custom's Union after independence. But common economic interests are what could strengthen relations on the China-Taiwan model where the different systems do not prevent economic relations. Lebanese banks are entering Syria and Lebanese bankers are very influential in Beirut. GAFTA is opening Syria, which is moving toward a service economy similar to Lebanon's that should attract Lebanese investment.

Comment by Sami Moubayed: Lebanon's identity is less Lebanese than sectarian, fragmented by region and sect. US-Saudi influence in Lebanon will constrain Syria-Lebanese economic relations. The terrorist attack in

Damascus had a Lebanese hand. The exchange of embassies is interpreted differently: for us it was to show we respected Lebanese sovereignty.

Comment: Lebanon cannot survive economically without Syria. But Syria managed the security relation poorly and we have found the Lebanese Chamber of Commerce is uninterested in economic relations with Syria. The grey economy of cross border movement to work and shop is significant but not investments.

EU-Syrian Relations (Maximiliano Trento)
The US-Europe alignment to isolate Syria, backed by Saudi Arabia, was discredited by its failure. Syria was able to remain steadfast by manipulating a multi-polar world, cultivating relations with Russia, China and Turkey. Implementing the Dubai model of a service economy allowed attraction of Gulf capital despite the Saudi attempt to isolate Syria. The 2006 Lebanon war and the 2008 Hizbollah coup in Beirut showed Europe that engagement with Syria could not be avoided. Europe also wants to see if it can manipulate Syria to isolate Iran and Hizbollah. Although neo-liberalism is discredited at home, especially by the financial crisis, the EU still tries to export it abroad.

Comment by Samer Lathikani: Europe looks at Syria through Israeli and Lebanese lens. The EU is also constrained by its US alliance: they followed the US policy of isolating Syria even though they did not fully agree on it. When Rice said the policy of the US on Syria was behaviour change, not regime change, this was the green light to Sarkozy to engage with Syria. Improvement in EU-Syrian relations resulted from the Turkey-mediated talks with Israel.

Comment: Europe failed in the region due to its excessive following of US policy. Syria-Europe trade is declining.

Syrian-Turkey Relations (Bulant Aras)
The Syrian-Turkey rapprochement is remarkable given Turkey's earlier alienation from the Arabs and Syria's perception of the Israel-Turkish alliance as a threat. The agreement over water helped, as both sides were able to share water and irrigate their lands. Turkey and Syria share common interests regarding the Kurds and Iraq. Turkey aims to stabilize the region against the threats of Iraqi fragmentation, US attack on Iran and unpopular US dominance in the region. The Turkish role in mediating with Israel is confined to conveying messages; there is still disagreement over the Syrian-Israeli border, with Israel wanting adjustments for security reasons.

The Syrian-Israeli Peace Process (Dr. Riyad Dawoodi, Syrian chief negotiator with Israel)

At the beginning of the 1990 Madrid peace process Israeli Prime Minister Shamir's strategy was to stall. Syria's attempt to coordinate the Arab position at the Madrid conference was frustrated by the PLO and Jordan who pursued their own interests. Later informal negotiations led to the "Rabin deposit" or guarantee that Israel would withdraw completely from the Golan, which allowed negotiations to go forward. These focused on Israel's security demands and reached a document on security principles. The Israelis also were bargaining over where the 4 June 1967 line actually was. Even though Rabin was assassinated, the Wye plantation negotiations in which the Israelis, Syrians and US were together in the same house looked optimistic until Peres went for early elections. There were suicide bombings in Israel and because Syria would not condemn them, this was used to disrupt the negotiations. Subsequently, under Netanyahu, the Israelis tried to renege on the Rabin Deposit. His slogan was "peace for peace," hoping to use force to impose a solution of the Palestinians and leave the Golan as an open issue to be bargained over. Ron Lauder, a Netanyahu friend, moved secretly between Israel and Syria and surprising progress was achieved without the involvement of the Americans; but this failed because the Israelis would not commit on the 4 June line. Barak was elected and the Shepardstown negotiations started. Barak said he would not deny or acknowledge the Rabin deposit and denied that UN 242 was relevant. There was bargaining over where the 4 June line was and Israel said it wanted more than its entitlement of the Golan waters under international water-sharing norms. Clinton hinted to Asad that he had good news and they met in Geneva in 2000 but Asad was given a map reflecting Israeli demands and he rejected it.

Like Hafiz, Bashar adopted peace as a strategic aim. After the Hariri assassination, the threat to Syria was severe and it was isolated. The 2006 Israeli war was to destroy Hezbollah and was also aimed at Syria. As it bogged down, Israeli military sources wanted to negotiate with Syria, but the US insisted the war continue. The post-war UN resolution on embargoing arms to Hizbollah will not be implemented without Syria's agreement. The war showed Israel's vulnerability and encouraged it to consider indirect negotiations with Syria as an alternative way to get security. We told the Israelis peace is the way to get security but the US did not want the Syrian track to proceed. Turkey intervened and conveyed the message from the Israelis that they were giving priority to the Syrian track.

The Syrian-Israeli Peace Process (Dr. Rizk Elias)
The context is that the opportunity for peace was lost in 1990 chiefly because Ehud Barak feared the political costs of removing the settlements from the Golan. Now the linkage of the Syrian-Israeli issue to other regional crises such as that over Iran makes it more difficult to reach peace. On the other hand, the Israel-Hizbollah conflict of 2006 was the first war when the Israeli interior was affected, showing it to be vulnerable. After that, Israeli demands in peace discussions were reduced: they concede the borders will be those of June 1967 and water rights will be negotiated. They want to keep Mt Hermon but we insist on total evacuation. However, Hizbollah cannot be used to challenge Israel again.

What kind of peace would likely result? The Israelis asked in the 1990s if Syria would sign a separate peace and Syrian negotiator Allaf said that if we did we still would not forget Palestine. The Golan is one of four tracks each of which may move at separate speeds. Syria would reach a "cold" correct peace with Israel separate from the Palestinians.

Comment of Tahsin Halabi (in charge of the Israel file at the foreign ministry). US policy under Bush meant the loss of the last eight years of the peace process. Nothing can be achieved until Bush goes. Syria's initiative with Turkey mediating with Israel was to neutralize the US. Various Israeli leaders have said in principle they would withdraw from the Golan, but this could have just been maneuvers.

Comment: I am one of those shocked at the Turkish mediation of peace talks with Israel. Why after our victory in Lebanon and the lifting of external pressures do we pursue this?

Syrian official responds: This is a mere dialogue, in the verbal stage of exploring the terms of reference and it has not become an input into actual decisions. Neither is this a big break in Syria's policy: when [in the 1990s] Israel expressed a willingness to withdraw to the 6 June borders we responded.

Comment: Syria has more credibility in talks with Israel because of Israel's failure to destroy Hezbollah in the 2006 war, because of US failures in Iraq and because of the emergence of Iran as a player in the Arab world.

About the Author

Samir Seifan is a prominent Syrian Economist. He holds a bachelor degree in economic sciences from Aleppo University/Syria (1974) and a diploma in finance from the Technical High School of Leipzig/Germany (1987). He is president of the Syrian Management Consultants Association (SMCA). He runs his own business as the Managing Partner of Arab Development Consultants (ADC), a firm providing economic research and business consultancy for the private sector, governmental institutions and international organisations. He has participated in several government teams for economic reform in Syria. He is the writer or co-writer of several books and studies about reform in Syria.

The St Andrews Papers on Modern Syrian Studies is published by the Centre for Syrian Studies, University of St Andrews, Scotland and distributed by Lynne Rienner Publishers, Boulder, CO, USA. The series remit is to publish cutting edge contemporary research and analysis on modern Syria, with the focus on the contemporary economic "transition" (reform) and on Syria's current security problems.
http://www.st-andrews.ac.uk/~wwwir/syrian/

We invite submission of unsolicited papers, particularly papers that report on current empirical research on Syria. Send paper submissions to series editor, Raymond Hinnebusch, School of International Relations, University of St Andrews, St Andrews, Fife, Scotland, KY15 7SP, U.K. or by e-mail to rh10@st-andrews.ac.uk.

St Andrews Papers on Contemporary Syria

OTHER BOOKS IN THE SERIES

Changing Regime Discourse and Reform in Syria
Aurora Sottimano and Kjetil Selvik

The State and the Political Economy of Reform in Syria
Raymond Hinnebusch and Soren Schmidt

Syria and the Euro-Mediterranean Relationship
Jörg Michael Dostal and Anja Zorob

Syrian Foreign Policy and the United States: From Bush to Obama
Raymond Hinnebusch, Marwan J. Kabalan, Bassma Kodmani, and David Lesch

Syrian Foreign Trade and Economic Reform
Samer Abboud and Salam Said

Syria's Economy and the Transition Paradigm
Samer Abboud and Ferdinand Arslanian